ABOVE. *The author dancing with women factory workers and soldiers during Peking's May Day festivities.* RIGHT. *Left, Li Tieh-Fei, right, Wang Lein-Yi, translators; center, Communist Party official Yu Shang-Ven.* BELOW. *Canton's Pearl River, formerly so clogged with sampans that it was nearly impassable.*

I SAW RED CHINA

I SAW
RED CHINA

by Lisa Hobbs

McGraw-Hill Book Company

NEW YORK TORONTO

LONDON SYDNEY

The excerpts in Chapter 13 from the September, 1932 issue of the *National Geographic Magazine* are used with the kind permission of the *National Geographic Magazine*.

Library of Congress Catalog Card Number: 66-14533
Second Printing
29091

For Jack

1

It was damnably hot.

Now only a trickle of a stream and a 100-yard bridge separated me from my goal—mainland China.

The time was spring, 1965, and the place Lo Wu, end of the line for the passenger trains which wind through the tropically lush, cluttered villages that sprawl from Hong Kong through the British New Territories to the border of China.

We piled out of the train, an undistinguished-looking handful of tourists, and made our way into the cool of a small whitewashed building. A British border official, nattily attired in khaki with gleaming leather trappings, indicated a wooden bench on a small roofed veranda. A German shepherd police dog trailed at his heels.

"You'll have to wait," he said. "The formalities take a little while."

A few yards from the bench was a high wire fence, too high to leap over, with a curving overhand that made climbing it impossible. Beyond it, a stream—an ordinary, lazy little stream with spring wildflowers along the banks—with nothing to indicate that it divided two worlds. Possibly it was once a river, for its banks were sharply cut and steep. Two Chinese women, in rough gray workclothes and black buns shining, eased their way down its sides in silence, gathering wild yellow lantana. They had an audience: on the other side of the stream a soldier in mustard-colored uniform idly watched them. The sweltering, shrieking harbor of Hong Kong, with its shops of brocade and jade, its opulent hotels and high-rise apartments, its tin-shack squatters and child beggars, lay to the southeast only two hours' train distance away. It could have been at the other end of the earth.

Here at Lo Wu, we had truly reached the end of the line; we sat in the humming, buzzing warmth that seemed hung in a state of suspension. The police dog, flopped over the doorstep and dozing; the green, gentle undulations of the hills down to the South China Sea; the scent of sun on damp soil and grass, and the wildflowers—such placidity was the very opposite of the turmoil I felt within me.

I was a reporter for an American newspaper. If I could cross the bridge, breach that stream, I would be the first newspaperwoman on the staff of an American paper to enter China since the Communist victory in 1949. My state of tension and sick excitement had little to do with what, to some people, might appear as a glamorous foreign assignment. For, in fourteen years as a reporter, I had covered racial riots in Singapore, famine in India, had been arrested and held in Egypt when the Nasser regime took exception to my cabled stories. After half a dozen trips around the world, foreign assignments can become almost routine. But there was nothing routine about the China assignment. From its inception two years earlier it had been a difficult, tedious, and precarious venture. As I sat on the bench looking at the border, I felt that if there was any justice, my labored, circuitous journey to this little bridge would surely not end, now, in defeat.

2

Two years earlier I had approached my editor on the San Francisco *Examiner* and suggested that he send me to China. I thought I might be able to get a visa to China simply because I was not, and am not, an American citizen, although employed on an American newspaper. At this time I was under the impression that newspaper reporters from most countries other than the United States could get a visa to China provided they were willing to wait a couple of years. This is not the case: until October, 1965, when over a hundred European journalists were suddenly invited in for an organized tour, only a comparative fistful of journalists from anywhere in the world had been allowed into China. In other words, my employment on any newspaper anywhere jeopardized my chances of getting a visa—but my employment by an American newspaper banned me as effectively as American citizenship banned my news media colleagues here. Australian citizens who are merely "tourists," however, have no difficulty getting visas good for three to four weeks' travel in China.

Only partially aware of this, and anxious to give the project a try anyway, I went to the State Department in Washington, and told them of my resident status as an alien and my proposed trip to China. They gave me nothing but encouragement. "We don't care how many resident aliens go to China," they said. Officers told me bluntly that such trips were one of the few sources of direct information they had for keeping in touch with developments within China. One of them, a former resident of China, grew quite wistful and waxed on about the beauties of the lake districts around Soochow and Hangchow. These were my first dealings with the State Department and I was more than mildly surprised at the gap that seemed to exist between individual attitudes and "official" thought. I was warned, however, that I could not be issued a reentry permit and, by traveling in China, would relinquish my automatic right to reenter the United

3

States. On the other hand, I was told that reentry would be merely a matter of going through a lot of tedious paperwork at some consulate outside the United States, and waiting there for a new entry permit to be granted. They stated unequivocally that a visit to China would not be prejudicial to reentry.

Some weeks later, following an assignment for the Hearst newspapers in Singapore, I flew on to New Delhi, and applied for a visa at the Embassy of the People's Republic of China. I frankly stated I was an Australian citizen and my occupation —reporter for the San Francisco *Examiner* and Hearst newspapers.

After returning to San Francisco from New Delhi, I started a one-way barrage to Peking of letters, cables, grinning passport photos, even pleas to Premier Chou En-lai. I even threw in letters to unlikely sources of help, such as the director of the Chinese Journalists Union in Peking. I don't even know if there is such a union but somewhere someone told me there is, so off went an air letter. I carried on this futile project for nearly two years, after which I decided that if I couldn't get into China legally I'd have to get in illegally.

In late 1964 I learned that an Australian firm, Orbit Travel Agency, organized group tours of the China mainland in cooperation with Luxingshe—China International Travel Service—the occidental version of Russia's Intourist Agency. Friends in Australia obtained application forms. I filled them out in San Francisco and mailed them back to Sydney, where they were remailed to the travel agency in Melbourne from a local address.

In applying a second time for a visa I did not say I had lived in California for ten years, had been a staff reporter for the *Examiner* for five years, was the wife of a Los Angeles-born American, Jack Hobbs, a schoolteacher, and the mother of two Americans, Crispin, eleven, and Jonathan, eight. Instead, on the Luxingshe form I stated I was a "writer," not a journal-

4

ist, a "freelancer," not employed, and a permanent resident of Sydney.

I am not any good at lying, or even telling what novelist Richard Hughes calls a "disproportionate story." Yet I falsified my visa application with ease and facility, even delight, completely unmarred by even the shadow of a scruple. Why? I think it's because paperwork and bureaucracy are not quite real to me. Years ago—I had crossed France from Italy and had forgotten to get a French visa and the customs authorities at Calais made me undress—I saw quite clearly that one should take this man-made colossus seriously. But the realization faded. The concept of bureaucracy has never entered my consciousness with the same reality that people or hummingbirds have, and in the end I gave up trying, deciding to give it a modicum of recognition, such as paying taxes, but, as for the rest, letting the devil take the hindmost.

As for my personal reasons in taking whatever risk was involved in deceiving the Chinese Communist authorities, they are as mixed and as ordinary as a garden salad. I like reporting, particularly about people. I am ambitious, too—a word that women usually shrink from, seeing ambition as a virtue in a man and a vice in a woman. When applied to a man, ambition usually means good old American initiative, ingenuity, responsibility; in a woman it connotes an abrasive, meddlesome quality. I think of ambition as a simple desire to achieve that excellence, no matter how modest, of which one is capable: in that sense I am most ambitious.

Furthermore, to get into China challenged my ingenuity. One can put many labels onto this motivation but in the last analysis it is just plain ego. I wanted to see with my own eyes the face of the new China and I wanted to come back and tell my own readers what I, and no one else, thought of this most thrusting and populous nation on earth, which rates less press coverage than a grade B movie in my own country. I had no illusions of turning up "news" stories on a three-week guided tour. But I did have the advantage of being free of some of the restrictions of politeness and prudence which presumably determine the tack taken by the three foreign correspondents who are regularly based in Peking. Perhaps most important, America had been my home for over ten years. I knew first hand the almost total silence at home on all aspects of Chinese life, not only in the daily press but in television coverage and glossy magazine reporting. A coast-to-coast public opinion survey taken in the United States in the late spring (sponsored by the Council on Foreign Relations) indicated that 28 per cent of the persons interviewed did not even know that China had a Communist government! To break this silence in the "popular" press with a series of articles bringing to Americans as much simple, factual information as I could gather about day-to-day life in China seemed a worthwhile project.

My visa for China—or at least the fact that I had been approved by Peking to enter with an Australian group of tourists—came only four weeks before my arrival in Lo Wu on the Chinese border. In the middle of April I flew from San Francisco to Sydney. There I obtained a new passport (the old one had been issued at the Australian Consulate in San Francisco) and an Australian vaccination certificate.

In Sydney my parents assured me, as they have over the years, that a Chinese prison would be my ultimate destination. Earlier, it had been an Indian prison, an Egyptian prison, etc., depending on where my assignments had taken me. To try to prevent this tragic end, my mother cut the American labels out of my clothes and my father attempted to cut the Americanisms out of my speech. Then I joined a group of ten Australian tourists at Sydney airport and flew to Hong Kong. There we went through the usual hassle: China Travel Service took all our passports, went through them with meticulous care, and then announced no visas had been received from Canton for any of us! They assured us they would

6

telephone us at our hotel when they heard anything—if they heard anything! With Myra Roper, an Australian writer on our tour, I returned the next day, filled in more application forms, provided more passport pictures. I lurked in the background, feeling within a hairsbreadth of success, and unwilling to do anything that might bring attention to myself.

Yes, it seemed our visas were ready. We were to leave from the Kowloon-Canton railway station the next morning. Our passports would be returned at the border. Goodbye and good luck!

I'm going to need it, I thought, for now, sitting at the border, every second that passed confirmed my fears that everyone else would cross but that I would be turned back. For the most routine cross check in Peking would turn up my earlier application for a visa and puncture my disguise as an ordinary tourist from my native Australia.

Now there was a little movement on the bridge. A handful of Chinese, their goods swinging from bundles on a bamboo pole, children strapped to the backs of both their fathers and mothers, crossed the bridge from China. On the Lo Wu side, a uniformed Hong Kong border policeman stood watching the Chinese side.

One by one our passports were handed to us: my long sought-after visa, two thin sheets of paper with a red star stamped in the center, was clipped inside. There was no stamp inside my passport—no telltale evidence to inform other governments that the bearer had been to China.

Then the border officer turned and signaled: we were free to cross. We moved forward, carrying our hand luggage: a leather-backed camera slipped from my damp hand. Only steps now: the others laughed and talked in high excitement; I held my breath. And now the British Union Jack fluttered behind me and the red flag of China with its five golden stars stretched full in the wind before me. Splashed against the whitewashed wall was a huge red star. Underneath, in a loosely fitted mustard-colored uniform, an armed member of the People's Liberation Army looked on indifferently. A part of the station was being rebuilt and workers had torn up the asphalted sidewalk. And so the first American staff newspaperwoman to enter mainland China came in hopping along the railway ties.

I've made it, I thought. I have gotten in and with a little bit of luck I'll get out. At that moment it seemed very simple and uncomplicated. I failed to take into account one thing—that I, too, had been living in America for ten years, isolated from the world of China. As a result I had almost forgotten that the Chinese are also plain people, human beings like everyone else, and I would be dealing with them directly: at this point they were still a statistic and a rather alarming one—700 million faceless, voiceless Communists.

Yet, how quickly the faces began to fill in and the human sounds to take shape and meaning as we moved through the long roofed walkways into the massive, cool Shumchun station. A group of soldiers, red and gold epaulets on their shoulders, stopped their conversation to look at us with interest; two nurses at the health station, white masks over their faces, caps over their black hair, glanced up with bright, brown eyes; as we entered the station we caught sight of the girl porters in navy blue sailcloth slacks and jackets, thick braids hanging to the waist.

It was here that I first saw many of the features of China today that were to become so familiar—the red ideographs in frames quoting Party Chairman Mao Tse-tung; the pastel drawings of him surrounded by bouquet-presenting children; the flower pots bursting with blooms, and the total absence of litter, with the sidewalks clean enough to eat off. I thought at first it was "staged." Later I realized I didn't see any railway station or public facility of any sort that was any less colorful or less clean during my three weeks of traveling in China.

There is no doubt that the station at Shumchun, barely three years old in its present state, is meant to impress the visitor. And it succeeds. Large, cool, clean with high ceilings and comfortable lounge rooms that sport hand-crocheted antimacassars on every armpost, Shumchun is China's best foot forward—the pace-setter for much of what is to come.

We went up the broad cement staircase to the second floor and were taken through customs—camera counted, typewriter checked—and just as efficiently we went through the money changers. I had changed my American dollars in Sydney for pounds sterling: now I changed my pounds into Chinese yuan. The rate is approximately 1 yuan to .45 U.S. cents (in this book, however, I have equated 1 yuan to half an American dollar for the sake of quick and easy calculation). Yuan, incidentally, is almost worthless outside China: it can be changed in Hong Kong but only at a loss.

Then a customs official led us to a small reception room to await our guides. A few minutes later they arrived—the three men who were to stay with us night and day throughout the tour, two of whom were to play important roles during my stay in China.

Every foreigner in China, even paying tourist groups, is there at the behest of the Chinese Government and is regarded as a guest. Whether you speak Chinese or not—as Jim Law, an Australian-Chinese member of our party did—you are met at each city by an interpreter. Groups are met by one interpreter and an official of the Communist party. If there are more than ten in the group, the interpreter and party official, and possibly a student interpreter, remain with the group throughout the tour. In addition, as the group goes from city to city, it is given the benefit of a second interpreter and a second party official familiar with the area. Any conversation—apart from the trivialities of baggage and tickets—is repeated by the interpreter to the party official who then replies. It hardly makes for free and easy conversation. Only when our party was scattered in a bus, plane, or train, or ambling through gardens on a sightseeing tour, would our interpreters bypass the party official and engage in direct conversation.

When the two interpreters and one party official who were to accompany our group entered the reception room I scarcely gave them a glance. I was too busy browsing through the pile of free literature provided by the Foreign Language Press. These free book and pamphlet stalls are to be found anywhere in those cities where foreigners might be gathered. These publications largely comprise full reprints, and comments on, the exchange of letters between the central committees of the Communist party of China and the Communist party of the Soviet Union, the first dated November, 1963. These letters deal with the major differences that have split Sino-Soviet unity, such as peaceful coexistence, revisionism, trade, and territorial boundaries. Filled with bitter charges and counter-charges, the Chinese have reprinted the letters with headings such as: "The Leaders of the CPSU Are the Greatest Splitters of Our Times" while the comments bear such titles as: "The Truth About How the Leaders of the CPSU Have Allied Themselves with India Against China."

When our guides arrived, I was unaware of the extent and total hopelessness of the language barrier in China, not to mention the restrictions and difficulties of travel from one city to another without official permission. The Chinese have no mobility at all: no one can simply go to a bus or train depot and buy a ticket and take off for another part of the country. A trip anywhere outside of your own city requires a special pass, and this is given only in the case of extreme family emergencies, vacations, or job transfers initiated by the state. Otherwise, you are stuck. Even foreigners require a government pass to leave town for an overnight stay, and passes for more than three days—I was later told by a banker in Peking—were rarely if ever given. Unaware of complications such as these, I regarded my guides' presence as primarily an attempt to keep us under surveillance—a Chinese form of plain-clothes policeman whose language facility would serve as an excuse for making sure we didn't see anything we weren't supposed to see. I had traveled through most of Asia alone and saw no need of a nursemaid and resented the implication that I would be told what to see and what not to see in the towns that we were slated to visit. With some foreboding, I realized that this time I had no choice but to submit. Within a few hours, I was to realize that my judgment regarding the essential function of the interpreters and party official was absurdly inaccurate.

The air was formal and official. Yu Shang-ven, the party official, wore a gray dress suit—the high-necked, breast-pocketed tunic that lends a uniformed air. Westerners often take this as a uniform. In fact, it is merely Chinese Sunday-best dressing. Sitting on the edge of his chair, his large teeth polished and protruding, Yu beamed as he made a vigorous speech of welcome.

Coolly, with deft grace and delicate choice of phrase, Li Tieh-fei, the senior interpreter, repeated it in English. His blue dress shirt was unbuttoned casually at the neck, a beige cashmere cardigan matched biscuit-colored slacks. Twenty-two-year old Wang Lien-yi, traveling as a translator for only the second time, sat on the sidelines and listened. I looked at the group with whom I was traveling—five men, five women, all many years older than myself. They were a mixed lot and of mixed political beliefs. One was a long-retired school principal; one a housewife in her mid-fifties blossoming out after years of child-rearing and housekeeping; two retired farmers; the Australian writer Myra Roper; an economist named Paul

Marowetz; and a seventy-nine-year-old engineer named Jack Clark (later on the tour, Jack remarked that Yu Shang-ven "looks after me as if I were his father." To this young Wang Lien-yi replied seriously, "It is because you are so old.").

Now we were taken downstairs to a restaurant. The table was laid with snowy linen, silver cutlery, and ivory chopsticks. We were offered beer or bottled orange drink with our six course Chinese meal—a custom that followed us throughout our tour. For the first time since leaving San Francisco's Chinatown I struggled with chopsticks.

Silently, Wang took my chopsticks and placed his hand delicately over mine:

"I will teach you," he said, so seriously that I was relieved to look up and see Yu beaming at me and waving his chopsticks with wild enthusiasm.

After dinner we went down to the train. I have never seen such a clean vehicle. Yu counted heads—a gesture I was to see him make a hundred times—and ushered us aboard. Although he must have made the trip a dozen times, his enthusiasm was boundless—and it remained so for the entire trip. We settled into the deep comfortable seats and stretched our legs on the footrests before us.

A shyly smiling young girl—who looked all of fifteen and turned out to be twenty-five—came down the central corridor with steaming mugs of tea in tall, lidded pottery cups. Inside, the leaves floated thick and green.

As smoothly as if it were floating, the train slid out of Shumchun. And at that moment, the public-address system, a feature of every railway car in China, struck up a full-throated chorus of *The Song of the Motherland*.

The verdant, rain-sogged countryside of China opened before me.

2

The train moved swiftly,

smoothly, northwest to Canton.

A soft rain fell. The scene was like a painting, fixed in time. Rice plants sprouted tender green; faces, as wind-worked as the soil, bent in timeless, fixed gestures over the land; wide coolie hats like little cupolas were reflected and reversed in the upswept curves of ancient village buildings that huddled in clusters along the railway track.

Whatever difference communism has made to the soul of China, I thought, it hasn't changed its face.

And that is how I felt as the train—sparkling clean from its third mopping since our departure from Shumchun—pulled into Canton three hours later. Journalists who had claimed that communism had changed China from top to bottom were guilty, I felt, of optimistic exaggeration. Certainly, the trains were impressive. They were comfortable, with foam-cushioned seats on each side of a central corridor, astonishingly clean, even charming with their potted ferns at the corridor's end. Desks, with a tasseled lampshade on each, had been placed in those sections where two seats faced the engine and two had their backs to it, forming a cosy nook for four. The train was on time, too, as it pulled into a railway station where the azaleas—pink, red, and cyclamen—bloomed as if in a conservatory. But once in the streets outside the station, there was no immediate evidence of radical social change.

Canton is an old city with foreign trade channeling through it from as far back as 200 B.C. Its face is worn and yellow-gray with age: congested alleys, with wooden doors opening into soot-blackened one-roomed homes; open-air fires on which cooking pots steamed; sidewalk stalls with swarms of women; masses of people, drably dressed and obviously poor, and the air irritated with the sounds of bicycle bells and impatient horns. Yet, there was something different about this Chinese city from other Southeast Asian cities; for now I pushed the puzzle to the back of my mind.

A translator named Chin met us at the station. Short, bouncy, he was the liveliest of all the translators we were to meet. He bundled us into a bus and we were off to the Love-the-Masses (*Aichun*) Hotel. There are only two hotels in Canton in which foreign visitors stay: the other—it was the better one, we were told—was packed with buyers attending the Canton Export Commodities Fair. Love-the-Masses wasn't so grim as it sounded. The elevator ran smoothly, the soft beds had spotless linen, there was toilet paper in the private bathroom, and a strong, individually packaged soap so antiseptic that it would drive away any germs within ten feet. One great advantage was that it lay alongside Canton's Pearl River.

Remembering the pictures I had seen of the Pearl River years ago, I turned to gloat at the scene—and experienced a rude shock. The river scene before me bore little resemblance to the old pictures. Then it was so cluttered with sampans that passage through at times was impossible. Millions of human beings lived, not unlike water-rats, on the steaming, sluggish

14

flow. There was no sign of the sampans now, except for a few tattered remnants that drifted downstream. Later, when I asked Li Tieh-fei about the sampans, he said that all except some 5,000 river dwellers had been moved into public housing projects and they would be rehoused by the end of the year. The river before me now flowed with traffic—ferry boats tooting in and out of passenger terminals; larger crafts with belching smokestacks; produce-laden barques poled along with rhythmic strokes by either a man or a woman and maybe both. Steam rose from the river, thick and bilious in the late afternoon sun. On the river's opposite banks, the city spread out into a silhouette of streaming chimneys and then on to the subtropical plains of Kwangtung Province. I embraced it with my eyes. Good heavens, I thought, you're really in China at last!

A white-coated bellboy arrived with a Thermos of boiling water. It was so large I wondered if he had brought it to fill the tub. Later, I learned that these flower-painted Thermos bottles, standing two feet high, are a feature of every hotel room in China. Filled with boiling water—and constantly replenished from the kitchen—they come complete with large, lidded pottery mugs and packages of green tea wrapped in tinfoil. The Chinese drink tea almost continuously: there is a lidded mug of hot tea to be seen on every desk or work bench. Providing a hotel guest with the makings for a cup of tea is an elementary courtesy throughout China.

How to lock the room? The boy at the desk on my floor looked downright hurt when I asked for the key: by his gestures he intimated he would take care of my things! But in what way, I wondered, as I left for a stroll downtown with Li Tieh-fei and Yu Shang-ven in tow to point out the sights. I needn't have worried, for if there is one country in the world where the tourist doesn't have to worry about losing his personal possessions, it is China. We were told that theft of

15

personal goods barely existed in China today—a remark that, initially, was greeted by polite, if not somewhat cynical, smiles. Yet every experience we had bore this claim out: within a week none of us were bothering to lock our hotel rooms night or day.

Now, strolling through the streets of Canton, I realized what it was that had puzzled me earlier after first leaving the station. There were no beggars on the streets, no poor devils crawling along, maybe armless or legless, pushing a tin cup before them. Nor were children roaming the streets like packs of rats as I've seen them countless times in India, scavenging among the refuse for something, anything, to eat: nor were there any children just sitting on the curb, as one sees them in Mexico, selling their oranges or onions while the church bells toll midnight. No adults, either, with trays of useless trinkets and eyes that smacked of despair pulling at one's sleeve and begging for a sale.

In fact, everyone seemed to be coming and going, everyone seemed to have something to do. Only along the river were there people leisurely strolling. This initial impression of cleanliness and order on the streets of China was reaffirmed in all six of the cities I visited. Where were the beggars? What happened to them when the new regime took over? When I asked, I was told that those who were educable were taught simple skills and absorbed into productive society: the hopelessly mutilated were taken into state institutions or were pensioned off under the care of a specially designated individual.

The question of the "disposition" of China's millions of beggars, either handicapped, mutilated, or retarded, is one that no inquiring mind can simply shrug off: it is one that few writers raise, however. The horrid suspicion exists that, in a society where there is no surplus of food and individual productivity is almost the sole reason for existence, annihilation would be the answer. I have no way of proving whether it was or wasn't. Like many other questions which surround precisely what happened when the Communist regime took total control, verifiable answers are simply nonexistent. I have no doubt, from all the effort Chinese society is visibly expending in labor today, that any beggars capable of productive work would have been made use of. As for the hopelessly mutilated, I do not know. From what I saw later, China has a sensitive, if not indulgent, social conscience toward the very young, the sick, and the aged, none of whom are "productive." The sick appeared to be extremely well cared for in the hospitals and sanatoriums that I visited, and the aged, both in the hospitals and strolling the streets carried themselves with dignity, almost hauteur. Productivity in China today does not appear to be the sole *raison d'être* of existence: I saw no evidence that ran counter to the explanation given to me—that the beggars were absorbed into the productive community or institutionalized.

Our walk had taken us to a street corner opposite the Pearl River. A massive billboard with a rifle-brandishing soldier caught my eye.

"What does it say, Li?" I asked.

"Be prepared," Li read. "Be on the alert to defend yourself against the aggressive American imperialists."

I was well aware that the Chinese, or at least the government of China, have regarded the United States as an aggressive, imperialistic nation for the past fifteen years. But reading about it in the security of my office or the comfort of my San Francisco home, and standing on a street in China with the accusation only feet away, are scarcely related experiences.

Did these people—riding by on their bikes, stopping to tie up a toddler's shoe, peering anxiously at the quality of the vegetables just like housewives all over the world—did they really believe the United States was planning an attempt to

17

seize their country? At the moment it seemed farfetched, propagandistic, somewhat ludicrous. It didn't by the time I left China: by then I had seen the other side of the coin—not that I came to believe that America was interested in invading China but simply because I gained some insight into the "image" that American activities in Asia have created.

The printed word in any newly literate nation is invested with a magic infallibility. Government posters, banners, newspaper stories, constantly urge the Chinese people "to be prepared to defend the homeland of China." Those who know the Chinese well say the most ordinary peasant has a fund of shrewd common sense, plus more than a dose of stubbornness. It is quite possible, even likely, that the "official" message of preparing to defend the homeland would have fallen on disinterested ears if it weren't for the government being able to offer the people "positive proof" of America's "aggressive" intentions—three downed San Diego–built camera-equipped spy planes, now on display in Peking, flights of American planes over the island of Hainan, the U.S. Seventh Fleet on year-round duty in the China Seas.

To the Chinese man-on-the-street, these American activities have been too close to his home shores for comfort; they portend no good. In every way they coldly indicate the "correctness" of the government's warnings. In every way, they strengthen the nation's over-all acceptance of the printed message. America's successful efforts to keep China out of the United Nations is offered as the ultimate proof of American "insincerity." I was to be told repeatedly that such activity had reduced the United Nations to little more than "a tool of American imperialism."

As to preparations for war within China, I saw no signs— no air-raid shelters, no sandbagging, no barbed wire. When I asked Li Tieh-fei about the fear of war, he gave me an official-sounding reply:

"Fear is a negative reaction. We will fight and to the death, all of us, men, women and children, if we are invaded. Otherwise, there's no point in wasting our time and energy worrying about something over which we have no control."

And Yu Shang-ven threw in:

"Certainly, we will never invade any country: that is determined by our socialist policy."

I have referred above to the Chinese man-on-the-street. How could someone like myself, unable to speak a word of Chinese, attempt to assess what the average "man-on-the-street" in China believes?

The opportunities of talking to any but a handpicked few are negligible. Indeed, in my 4,000-mile tour by bus, train and plane I spoke directly to no more than forty English-speaking Chinese. Nor is facial expression necessarily an indication of state of mind or soul: only ten years ago the Chinese laughed and danced at funerals. Nonetheless, there are available clear-cut indications of the direction in which China's fast-moving social current is running. The masses of any nation move with the current, a small percentage through conviction, the majority either through indifference or lack of any alternative. (For instance, only 3 per cent of China's total population are actually members of the Communist party. A similar 3 per cent of the total population of the United States engaged in small or large political chores for their favored candidate during the 1964 presidential campaign.)

I sought to discover the currents in China not only by using my eyes and ears but by asking our interpreters for translations of every banner seen, every play attended, the movie advertisements that are outside every theater or plastered in glassed-in frames along the sidewalks, the songs the children sang, and, most important, the contents of the *Peking People's Daily*—a slim tabloid on tissue-thin white paper. At no time did I have any reason to question the absolute honesty and accuracy of the translations given. There was never any hesitation that smacked of pussy-footing nor any attempt to present statements of any kind—of a personal or political nature, either spoken or on banners—in the most agreeable form. If a speech was made that was delicately phrased, that is how it was presented to us: if a banner was brash and aggressive, so was the translation. Further, there was an Australian-Chinese, Canton-born Jim Law, in our group: he verified my hunch that we were receiving exact and undiluted translations.

This was Jim's first trip back to China in a life that had included some years in several of the world's Chinatowns, including New York's. In his twenties he had emigrated to Australia, where he and his Australian wife, Elva, a dainty redhead, owned a restaurant in Melbourne. They were the parents of two teen-age daughters.

After our walk downtown, we returned to the hotel. After sundown, we boarded the special bus provided in every city by Luxingshe for tourist groups and went to the Tai-Ping-Guan restaurant. Canton is famous for its food and pastries, and this was the most lavish restaurant we were to visit. At the Tai-Ping-Guan, in an opulent setting of heavily carved teakwood furniture, brush-stroke scrolls and golden screens, we dined on stuffed crab, boneless duck-webs with mushrooms, braised chicken with *pu-ning* bean paste, big skirt shark's fin, roast rice-ear birds and water-chestnut pudding.

Like all countries, China offers its best to the foreign visitor. He eats in the swankiest dining rooms of the poshest new hotels, he is taken everywhere by cab or in a private bus equipped with desks and lampshades; his hotel rooms with private bath could be home for two Chinese families. This fosters the notion, often expressed, that anything at all good in China is the exclusive property of foreigners, that the Chinese themselves are shut out of it. What I saw at the Tai-

Ping-Guan restaurant argued to the contrary. It was packed with hundreds of young Chinese couples eating out with their children. The food they were eating was certainly plainer than ours and the furniture in the massive rooms was cheap and utilitarian. But they were being waited on, they were, in every sense of the word, "dining out." They were enjoying, as we enjoyed, the pleasure of eating food one hasn't had to buy and prepare oneself, the pleasure of the company of others, the pleasure of the physical surroundings, for all the rooms opened onto a classically styled inner courtyard with stream, camel-back bridge, rookery, and weeping willow. This restaurant, which runs the length of a city block and is three stories high, feeds 15,000 persons a day.

It was the first time I had seen and heard the Chinese at play. Remember, I had been in China only one day: the sense of ebullient vitality, the din of unrestricted noise and laughter was nothing short of astonishing.

Our translators joined us at this dinner—a rare occurrence —and during the seven-course meal we learned a little of their private lives.

Wang Lein-yi, serious, soft spoken, told me he was not married and did not plan to be until "at least thirty."

(The legal age for marriage is eighteen for girls, twenty for boys. At present the government is considering raising it, primarily as a birth-control measure, to thirty for men and twenty-five for women.)

Wang, who ate delicately, carefully, resting both hands in his lap between courses as if mindful of some training, said he lived in a room outside Peking. Rent cost 1 yuan (50 cents) a month and food, 12 yuan ($6) a month. As Wang earned 50 yuan ($25) a month, this pointed up one of the curious economic facts of life in China today—a fiftieth of one's earnings goes to rent, while one-fourth is spent on food.

Wang added a note that I was to hear often and always

with the same modest pride: he could save from his salary and possessed one of the first bank accounts in his family's history. Next year, as his English improved, his salary would be increased by 10 yuan ($5) a month.

Chin, the interpreter from the Canton branch of Luxingshe, had a totally different personality from Wang: quick in his movements, he bounced from one task to another as lively as a cricket, shouting into telephones, enjoying a joke with relish and laughter, interpreting with clear-cut vigor. He glowed as he told of China's success that day in the Asian table tennis championships—the Chinese are most enthusiastic about sports and ping-pong rates high.

Chin, in a rare revelation—for the Chinese do not usually wish to discuss their personal life or any aspect of it—said he was married, had no children, and his wife was a doctor of traditional (Chinese) medicine. Traditional medicine requires six years of intensive study, with particular emphasis on neurology. Chin said he and his doctor-wife lived in one room of an apartment building, sharing the kitchen and bathroom with several other families.

Asked how he had won his wife, he laughed. Hard to say whether the laughter was one of amusement or embarrassment: obviously, the question was an unexpected one! He replied by saying he had not asked her parents, or anyone's, permission to take her first for walks, then later to the movies. Someone in the group asked Chin if his wife was pretty: he brushed the question aside, again with a laugh. I was to notice time and time again that the question of personal beauty and attractiveness is regarded in China as somewhat superfluous, perhaps a little vulgar, and certainly one that is outside the area of public discussion.

"When you decide to marry," said Chin, "you go to the central office and sign a certificate. No promises are made. The card is merely proof of marriage. If you want to you can have friends in to celebrate."

22

I asked Chin what had happened to the former owner of the restaurant. There was a brief, earnest discussion with the maître d' and the waiter, and then I was told that he was working elsewhere and that he was one of the "national capitalists" of China. These are the former owners of some 70,000 private enterprises that became state-owned when the state seized all private industry in 1956. The state agreed to pay all former owners 5 per cent on their capital investment for ten years. At the same time, the national capitalists were subjected to an all-embracing reeducation program designed to dispose them to "remold themselves conscientiously to become builders of the new society." (The quotation is from a statement made later by Professor Yung Lung-kuei, an economist with whom I later spoke in Peking.)

After we left the Tai-Ping-Guan we returned to Love-the-Masses, where a surprise awaited me. During dinner, I heard Jim and Elva Law discussing plans to visit his relatives in Canton. Frankly, I wondered if Jim and Elva would be welcome, if there wasn't such a thing in China as "guilt by association," if, in fact, their relatives would be just as pleased if Jim and Elva stayed away. As it turned out, my ruminations couldn't have been further from the truth. Jim and Elva not only visited whenever and wherever they wanted, but the warmth of the welcome they received was such that they always returned.

Encouraged by Jim's plans, I told Li Tieh-fei when we returned to the hotel that I wanted to go for a walk. His reply was to warn me not to get lost. I must have looked a bit incredulous as I asked again if I could go wherever I chose. Certainly, said Li, but don't fall in the river!

This didn't at all jibe with what I had expected. There were to be no restrictions at all on my wanderings within any of the cities we were to visit. Only once did my announced intention of going for a walk arouse any interest. Apparently, that was because the interpreter looking after us had been

23

roused from her bed at midnight on one occasion to rescue a Swede whose nocturnal wanderings had landed him, lost and bereft, in the local police station.

I took full advantage of freedoms that, even three years before, had not been permitted. Some salesmen with whom I later spoke in Peking said that, five years ago, they could not leave their hotels. All that has now changed. With every trip, they told me, there are greater freedoms.

Certainly, I experienced no restrictions as to when and where I wandered. I went for walks at sunup, noon and night —I wandered in and out of markets, poked my nose into backyard factories, mingled with crowds sunning in the park, and on a couple of occasions tried out a few polite Chinese expressions on English-speaking university students. Not once did I have any reason to believe I was being watched or followed.

"Ah, but an Occidental sticks out like a sore thumb in the Orient," I was told on my return to the United States. "There is no need to trail you. The Chinese authorities knew at every moment precisely where you were."

I replied that certainly, with 4,000 foreign buyers in Canton alone, such a network of shadowing and tailing would go a long way to providing work for China's millions.

"Anyway, what would I be doing?" I asked curiously.

"Passing microfilm, of course," I was told seriously.

That night, as I strolled alongside the Pearl River, mingling with hundreds taking the cooler night air, I gained some insight into what is meant by the claim that China has been changed from top to bottom. The gutter is "home" to no one in China today. It is possible to walk the streets without stepping over bodies: it is possible to move around without shame and guilt. I know of nowhere else in Asia where this is true.

3

Canton doesn't rate too highly,

in my estimation, as a tourist city. But snippets from the four days I spent there are worth reporting simply because, unimportant and unrelated though they might appear, they are part of the myriad pieces that make up today's China scene.

Our first visit was to the Lan Pu nursery, where fifty varieties of orchids were on display. None of them were in bloom, however, and we were reduced to looking at identical green sticks in identical red pots while Chin assured us of their magnificence, had we come at the right time. It was my first visit to a Chinese garden and I wandered around in the misty rain, enchanted with the pavilions, willows, lotus-covered ponds, twisting little paths. In one path I came across a gray stone marker with hewn ideographs. I asked Wang what it said: it was a poem by Marshal Chu Teh, one of the leaders of the 5,000-mile Long March in 1934–35. It was the first of many poems, including some by Chairman Mao, that I was to see on display in China.

I asked for a translation, trying to imagine whether poems by members of the Joint Chiefs of Staff would add or detract from the beauty of our own American parks! Wang peered, muttered to himself, and finally grinned with some embarrassment. At first, it appeared, he couldn't understand it: ideographs, even to the Chinese, are not always immediately recognizable.

The meaning of the poem was too ephemeral for translation, however. Wang struggled but finally threw up his hands in a hopeless gesture, looking shy at his failure. It was my first encounter with the peculiar difficulties that sometimes surround the translation of Chinese into English. Later, I found an excellent example to illustrate this point. "Bamboo in your chest!" is the Chinese expression for "Take courage" or "Be brave!" but, if translated literally, it is "Have sticks in your stomach!"

Next door to the garden, over the massive seven-year-old Canton Gymnasium, flew a red banner:

"Proletarians of the country unite!"

Through the windows of the building, which looked old and illkept for its age, young men in red T-shirts and boxing gloves could be seen prancing around punching bags.

We crossed the broad paved boulevard to Yueh Shiu Park. Set back, but in the center of the main entrance where it hits the oncoming visitor, is a permanent brick wall bearing, in gold ideographs on red, the message:

"Long live Chairman Mao."

After looking through an extensive bonzai tree exhibition which, incidentally, had attracted a large audience of workers in shorts and thongs, and mothers with small children, as well as individual schoolchildren apparently on their way home from classes, we went up the misty hill to the Canton Museum.

This is an imposing old building, five stories high and dominating a hill, with a curving emerald green roof and gold trimmings on its red front. But there is hardly a thing in it. Its

26

vast empty halls are a profoundly sad sight. There are a few genuine pieces of iron- and brasswork and pottery, but most of the pieces on show are merely copies. Even the souvenirs of pre-Liberation peasant uprisings—the flag used by the peasants in the commune uprising against the British in 1841, for instance—are copies. There are some blurred and faded pictures of Chairman Mao and rebel leaders as they were when they organized the Communist party in Canton forty years ago. But of China's great culture and ancient arts there is practically nothing.

It was my first intimation of the extent to which China has been looted and pillaged, and her cultural heritage sold out piece by piece to the highest bidder, for centuries. Time and time again I was to visit museums that were, by any metropolitan city standards, bereft of possessions. China's art is scattered in private collections or museums throughout the world, or hidden in the caves of Taiwan. Only recently have long-hidden treasures been yielded up from the recent excavation of the Underground Palace of Ting Ling at the Ming Tombs outside Peking and these have boosted somewhat the country's cruelly depleted cultural possessions. In the main, however, the only thing that the Japanese or Nationalist forces left behind were four- and five-feet high jade carvings too heavy to move.

The museum overlooks the city stadium with its 50,000 seats and two Olympic-size pools, another post-Liberation product (Liberation, of course, refers to the end of 1949, when the last Nationalist troops were driven from the China mainland by Communist forces). This stadium and pools were high in the Yeh Shiu Park in a natural basin ringed by hills; the site, selected with obvious care, reflected the high place in which the Chinese hold competitive sports. I was to see a score of firstrate stadiums and pools, but was told that the really "in" sports activity in China today is "conquering" mountain peaks and swimming in rough seas and turbulent rivers.

After leaving the park we piled into our bus and were driven back to Love-the-Masses Hotel. These buses, built in China, varied in comfort. Those used for short runs were like city buses anywhere, with plastic seats and inclined to be hard. The buses used for long runs—and the buses used all the time in Peking—were marvelously comfortable, an ideal way to travel. Well-sprung and built high, their curved glass fronts provided an unhindered view; the foam-rubber seats, covered with an antimacassar for both hands and head, were scrupulously clean. In each bus there would be a desk where the seats faced both front and back, providing a nook for the note taker or map surveyor, and there was a tasseled lamp for trips that went beyond daylight hours. The drivers were careful and given to neither horn honking nor gear grinding. I noticed that the young girls who seem to comprise the bulk of China's taxi drivers also drove with some respect and understanding of the mechanics involved.

Back at the hotel, we had dinner in the eleventh-floor dining room. Our dining room, off another room in which both Chinese and foreign guests were eating, was semiprivate. Our translators and officials ate in a third dining room where the rather bare, utilitarian atmosphere and the uniformity of navy blue denim worksuits suggested that it catered mainly to thinner pockets.

Each morning, we were to be asked whether we wanted to eat Chinese or Western food that day: either way, eating in China was always a pleasure. Food for the tourist, at least, is plentiful and varied. If Western food was ordered the meal included hors d'oeuvres, soup, fish, the main course, dessert, and fruit with coffee. The fish course included a wide variety of shellfish, while steak or chops usually comprised the main meat dish.

If Chinese food was ordered, anything could be expected —cold roast duck, hot chicken, fried perch-balls, snake soup with wildcat meat, scrambled fresh milk, turtle sauté, and egg tarts or minced meat biscuits for dessert. For the first few days of the tour, we sat around politely waiting for the dishes to be passed from one to another: after a week we all served ourselves Chinese style, standing and stretching across the table one after another. We'd seldom all be sitting at the same time. Miss one item and the waiter or waitress descended with an inquiring look: was something wrong? Young girls, looking in their late teens but most likely in their twenties, comprised the bulk of the table help. Usually they wore white jackets over navy slacks, but in Peking's elegant Nationalities Hotel they looked very European with thick black stockings, black frocks, and white, ruffled pinafores—everything but caps!

On the second day in Canton we visited an ivory factory and the Canton Export Commodities Fair.

The ivory factory is a multistoried building over a shop on one of Canton's main streets. It employs a couple of hundred persons and, we were told, has tripled in size since Liberation. Prior to that time, girls were not taught the trade for fear they would marry and pass the secret of their father's skill out of the family. As a result, only a handful of men qualified as ivory carvers. Today the employees range from teen-age girls to old, bent, bespectacled men who engrave classical poems, under a magnifying glass, on the sides of two-inch letter seals. For export, these seals are still a popular *objet d'art*.

We were told that this factory was formerly the only source of all the carved ivory that had come out of China formerly. Certainly, the highly ornate carved pieces looked like the sort of thing that one's great aunt treasured many years ago. The simple, clean lines of modern art—or of some of China's ancient porcelain pieces, for that matter—have in no way modified the ivory products of the new China. They are as intricate, ornate and dust-catching as ever—pagodas, with scores of little bells; richly carved ships; floral encrusted balls-within-balls—just as they were produced hundreds of years ago.

The factory conditions were good; however, this factory is a regular part of the visitor's guided tour. We started in the ill-lit basement where curving ivory tusks were stacked on the dirt floor and old women sat over tubs of water dipping and polishing the finished products until they developed a mellow patina. Then we wound our way up to where scores of workers bent over their benches scratching away at the ivory with pencil-like razor-edged tools. The workers were all casually dressed: the Cantonese, probably because of the hot climate, dress more informally than the residents of other cities we visited. These workers wore navy shorts and a T-shirt with or without a sports shirt. Some wore shoes without socks and some sandals and thongs.

Here there was ample natural lighting and the louvered windows caught the afternoon breezes that blow through the hot city. The girls wore floral cotton blouses and navy cotton slacks. Like their Western counterparts, they had tried to beautify their surroundings with flower pots on their desks. Everyone worked with a steaming mug of green tea beside him.

I wanted to take a picture of a couple of young girls and asked Li Tieh-fei to see if they objected. Before he had done this I changed my mind.

"If you ask them, Li, they'll probably feel they have to say yes."

He looked puzzled and asked why.

"Because you're kind of official," I said. I really meant it: I was sure even a simple request like this might be a little intimidating coming from a member of an official group.

But Li laughed outright; he seemed genuinely amused.

"They'll say no if they don't want to," he said. He thought my notion very funny.

The workers themselves designed their final product. They follow—in their head without any sketches—basic designs but they are allowed, and we were told encouraged, to make changes and innovations. They are given a slab of elephant tusk: it is their sole responsibility to produce a salable work of art from it. I noticed here, as I did in all work that required sensitivity and skill—and even among children at play—the extraordinary, slim beauty and dexterity of the Chinese hands. The girls, in particular, are graceful to their fingertips. Their plain clothing, lack of makeup and jewelry, do nothing to detract from this sense of grace.

We couldn't buy any of the goods on display in the shop downstairs. Almost all nonessential goods being produced in China are exported abroad in return for basic commodities.

Later, we went to the Export Commodities Fair where over 15,000 items are on permanent display. We were told that 3,000 new items had been added by China's burgeoning industry over the past twelve months. Some 4,000 foreign buyers—from Japan, Great Britain, various African nations, Canada, France, East Germany, Australia, and South America —were in Canton to visit the fair, the seventeenth held since the ten-story, city-block-long building went up in 1959.

The exhibition itself covers four floors: the heavy construction machinery and buses are displayed in a courtyard to the rear of the building. Beyond that is a large warehouse for carpets. The smaller products, such as jade carvings, silk embroidery, human hair, antibiotics, precision instruments, are displayed in glass cases.

On every floor, in the lobby by the elevators and in scores of private conference rooms, foreign buyers could be seen sipping tea in armchair comfort and signing contracts.

On one floor there was a photographic exhibition includ-

31

ing stills from Chinese movies, which are tremendously popular. To get into any show night or day entails the purchase of a ticket (which costs 30 to 40 cents) five days or so in advance. From these stills, and from the pastel posters outside the numerous movie houses and in billboard type advertising, it was apparent that most movies are either about the Viet Nam war, the Japanese occupation, or the Civil War.

A modest-sized—perhaps thirty-three inches square—black and white picture of the explosion of China's first atomic bomb was on display.

"Our bomb," said our guide, two words, but eloquent with pride.

I peered at the picture with mock *expertise* and then, unable to resist the chance of spoofing the childish bellicosity of the international scene, replied quietly:

"Our bomb is bigger than your bomb."

Curiously, this was to be the only time in my three weeks in China that I saw any reference, either photographic or verbal, to China's atomic power.

Later that day we piled into the bus and went to a hot springs resort about three-hours' drive from Canton. High in the wooded hills, close to a broad river swollen with spring rains, is a cluster of new and modern hotels. They are separated one from the other by paved walks, curved stone bridges, brackets of fern and bamboo forests. The hotel in which we stayed had vast bedrooms: mine was 18 by 24 feet and let onto an enclosed veranda with rattan shades and a magnificent view of the surrounding hills. There were slippers under my bed—the polished floor was scattered with rugs and the tub in my private bathroom was sunk four feet into the floor. Into it spurted the natural hot spring waters.

Outside everything was fresh and wet from the spring rains. To wander through the little bamboo woods, to pause on an old gray stone bridge, to hear the thin, high voice of a

Chinese girl singing across the fields to her friends, were perhaps ordinary events in themselves. To me, they were invested with a sense of melancholy and apprehension. For the loneliness of the woods, the isolation of the resort, and of course the sight of troops bivouacked on the hills near the bridge, thrust home sharply the realization that, if I was not exactly in "enemy" territory, I was certainly in an indefensible position. My worst fear was not that the Chinese authorities would somehow discover I was a reporter for an American newspaper, but that this discovery might lead someone in Peking's bureaucracy to suspect some State Department link or affiliation, and delay my departure from China indefinitely.

The following day we were scheduled to visit a nearby waterfall. We set off early in a slight, intermittent drizzle. The bus wound up the hills on yellowed, muddy roads: finally, it could go no farther. Umbrellas were produced and we got out of the bus and set off in a steadily increasing downpour. At any moment I expected the tour to be canceled: but, no, we wound steadily up a thin mountain path as the drizzle turned into a torrent. We were getting a firsthand lesson in China's water problem!

Some of the Australians turned back. Now we were left with one Chinese plus one umbrella apiece to protect us. Up and up we went, slipping and sliding along the thin rocky ridge; the stream was now roaring as it fell away beside us and the rain was of blinding force. With totally unperturbed smiles, with their gray tunics soaked in black patches, our hosts beamed us on. Finally, we reached the head of the falls. The rugged gray-slate rocks and booming water threw up a fine mist: through it we stood and grinned triumphant one at the other. Now, satisfied that we were satisfied, our guides returned us, like so many sponges, to the bus.

Back at the hotel we learned that, although it was only noon, there would be no electricity until 6 p.m. We were told that the hydroelectric plant on the nearby river was undergoing repairs. The corridors and rooms were plunged into gloom. Down the hall I could hear Phil Howell, a grayhaired Australian businessman and bachelor, shouting, "No, no." There was a banging around in his room, then he poked his head out the door, red-faced and laughing. Behind him stood a little maid with a Dutch bob and a puzzled expression.

"She keeps tugging at my pants," he shouted. "She wants to take them off and dry them. Can you find a translator to tell her I can't take them off while she's here?"

The young maid's attitude was typical of the approach the Chinese have toward the ordinary human functions. There is none of the self-consciousness of the West, although there is a great deal of modesty evident. But their modesty doesn't surround the usual objects of the West, such as the bed or bosom (which in China appear to have no connotation other than being just that—a piece of furniture or a functional part of woman's anatomy). Rather it seemed to be directed toward any idea of personal goals and aspirations, and ambitions. I was to be told a score of times by young Chinese girls that they truly hoped they could contribute to their country's progress and were willing to do any task asked of them—never that they had any more personal aspirations. But if you walked into the women's toilet on a commune or campus— the latrines slits in the ground and all the girls astride struggling with their slacks and the pajama-like cord that holds them up, they'd beam a welcome from their ungainly position and cheerfully greet you with a "Hello, Aunt." (Teen-agers and children call all adults "Uncle" and "Aunty." There is no equivalent to "Ladies and Gentlemen" and this, too, is translated as "Uncles and Aunties.")

Back in the hotel that day, the girls finally got all the pants collected and gathered them triumphantly at the end of the corridor. There, they took an iron that looked like a relic from the iron age and filled it with hot coals from a foot-high burner. It worked just as well as a steamiron and the men returned to Canton dry and creased.

That night, we went to the People's Cultural Park in Canton to see the acrobatics, for which the Chinese are traditionally, and rightly, famous. The open-air theater, with seating for perhaps 2,000 persons, is situated in the 10-acre park in the center of the shopping district. It was packed with middle-aged and older workers. There were many young people, couples with children, but a noticeable absence of young single people. Later, after becoming better acquainted with China's younger generation, I realized they are probably too busy with night classes and political meetings to take much time out for pure entertainment.

There were two empty rows in the front: shortly after the performance started these were filled with some forty foreign buyers from East European countries. No sooner were these seated, than a group of Chinese workers arrived late; seats were promptly set up for them in front of the buyers! I noticed time and time again that, although the Chinese are consistently polite and helpful to foreigners, they are no longer subservient to them: their own needs, at least in such public places as the theater, are answered with equal consideration.

It was during intermission that Myra Roper and I asked Chin and Li if we could see a few moments of the modern Peking opera which was playing in a theater across a tree-lined walk.

We stood in the back row in the darkness.

There, on the stage, were two soldiers. One, a Chinese, stood with a bayonet-fixed rifle in his hand. At his feet, cringing on his knees, was a captured GI. The GI clasped his hands, trembled so violently his fear was visible to us in the back row. The Chinese soldier spoke, made a threatening thrust: the GI whined for mercy. The audience shook with laughter.

I was speechless with anger.

35

"Well, how did you like it?" said Chin, as fresh and chirpy as ever.

Myra muttered something politely; I couldn't find my voice.

But on the way home, I told Li Tieh-fei that I had spent some years living in America and never, never, NEVER had I seen one Chinese picked on because of his nationality and subjected to such crude, base, and offensive ridicule.

Said Li:

"The audience was amused because only today another American pilot was shot down in Viet Nam carrying, as they all do, a document asking in several different languages that his life be spared. We cannot understand such cowardice," he said.

I felt the statement beneath contempt and beyond comment and said so. Yet my surface anger was only part of what I felt at that moment: there was fear and despair in my heart —fear that the Chinese will make the awful mistake of truly believing that Americans are cowards, and despair at the consequences of this error in judgment.

We were now in the lobby of Love-the-Masses Hotel.

I turned and looked at Li.

"I could have written that play myself," he said.

I went up to bed: there was nothing more to be said.

4

The rain, which had plagued us
continuously since our arrival, kept up a steady downpour.
Even the handful of people who would pause for a moment
opposite Love-the-Masses Hotel to see the foreigners trooping
in and out of their buses and cabs were nowhere to be seen as
we set off for the Hudong Renmingangshe, the East Flower
People's Commune. The Western-garbed foreigner, despite
his increasing familiarity in China now, is still good for a
moment's diversion.

Ten-minutes' ride from the hotel we were in the lush,
semitropical agricultural land of Kwangtung Province. It was
Sunday, but in the rice paddies, calf-deep in mud, peasants
bent to their labor unconcerned. Sunday is not a day of rest in
China: all workers get one day a week off but they don't
necessarily pick Sunday. Women, including those on the
communes, get six days a month off. Wide coolie hats and
cloaks made of woven palm leaves offered the workers some
protection against the rain which threatened to turn the un-
paved road into a muddy morass. Other workers sought protection against the mud walls of roadside shelters.

Our bus stopped outside what was formerly an old temple.

Shao Ying-paio, a tall, boyish looking farmer, introduced himself through our interpreters as the director of the commune and led us into a pavilion-type hall. Three fluorescent lights burned in the 25-foot ceiling; cups of steaming green tea were laid on the thick plastic cloth of the long, banquet-size table. I was anxious to get moving: at least I'd made it to one commune! But after only three days in China I knew that the formalities of welcome must be observed. I settled down to drink tea and crack the peanuts which, we were told, were part of the commune's crop.

"We were very happy to have you visit our commune and on behalf of the management committee and all members of the commune I would like to extend a welcome," said Shao.

This was translated by Li Tieh-fei.

"Especially for coming in the heavy rain," Shao added with a beaming smile.

Shao said the 13,300-acre commune was established in October, 1958, by the merging of sixty cooperatives in two townships. These cooperatives totaled 11,868 families—or 51,051 persons. Of these 48,000 were "agricultural." Of this number 21,511 persons were in the labor force and the rest were children and old people.

A little while later Shao said that the work load was divided among 365 production teams, each of 100 persons.

When I protested that this meant a labor force of some 36,000 persons, an animated five-minute discussion followed in very earnest Chinese. At the end of it, Li, looking as bewildered as I felt, looked up and said:

"Yes, that is so."

I wanted to pursue it but when I opened my mouth a loud snore drew my attention to one of the Australian tourists, Charles Roberts of Horsham, who, oblivious to everything, slept soundly in an armchair. The other tourists, in varying stages of despair, were looking at me.

38

I don't believe for a moment that director Shao was deliberately misleading us: either he had left some vital figure out, something had been lost in translation, he was weak on mathematics, or possibly my hearing was failing. This simple incident was my initiation into the extraordinary difficulty in obtaining facts and figures in China that add up and make sense under analysis. All writers who go to China complain of the same thing. It is usually a total waste of time to voice your objections: you will find yourself the only one annoyed or astonished that the figures don't quite pan out.

I was just reconciling myself to the labor discrepancy when we were given a breakdown of the commune's income and expenditure. Production costs were 40 per cent (I would have liked an explanation of this as it is extraordinarily high considering there are no labor costs); 5.7 per cent went to other investments; 5.4 per cent taxes; 3 per cent to a general welfare fund; 6 per cent on administration costs, and 44.6 per cent on distribution costs. This adds up to 104.7 per cent!

In some irritation and despair I whispered, through our interpreter, to Yu Shang-ven. He grinned when I complained that it didn't make much sense: it apparently didn't to him either. Later he said that perhaps I should remember that some "simple" people weren't used to figures.

I think Yu's attitude summed up the Chinese attitude well: if everyone is doing his best, what do the figures really matter? Furthermore, is it really the foreigner's business anyway?

By now Shao was explaining how the team system works.

"Each team decides what it can accomplish," said Shao. "The brigade leader is part of the team and they discuss with him whether their goal is fair or not.

"It would not be possible for a team to decide to produce wheat if rice were needed, for instance. The brigade leader helps them work out a plan so all can benefit."

39

Shao said that wages paid each production team vary in each commune and even within each team, workers receiving different pay according to their productivity.

"Each kind of work has a different set of measurements," said Shao. "The output is checked by other members of the production team."

It sounded a cumbersome way of making up a payroll, particularly when wages are paid only once a year in a lump sum, but, if Shao's beaming approbation were any indication of the system's workability, it appeared to be a success.

Shao said that delegates to a representative conference are elected annually in competitive voting.

"These delegates then decide how much will be paid back to the workers in wages and how much put back into the commune for reinvestment.

"My native town is quite close to this commune," said Shao. "Before Liberation, this area was very poor and constantly plagued by natural disasters, such as alternate drought or flood. There was no water conservation whatsoever and production was very poor. Thousands of persons lived from crop to crop on the verge of starvation.

"Sixty-nine per cent of the land was owned by the landlords, who comprised 4 per cent of the population. Eighty-four per cent of the population had only 9 per cent of the land. And half the products of that 9 per cent had to be paid back to the landlords as rent. Many of the people had to borrow money just to survive the bad years: then their profits during the good years all went to pay the interest. They could never hope to pay back the capital."

A score of questions popped into my mind. How was the merging of the cooperatives accomplished, or to go back a year or two earlier, under what conditions did the peasants give up land to which they had barely gained title after years of the most oppressive serfdom by warlords and landlords?

Some small landowners in Kwangtung Province were executed for refusing to cooperate when the Communist party took over. Pictures of them being led, roped, to their place of execution while villagers watched were widely distributed, with full approval of the party, all over the world.

Shao must have been a boy at this time and I longed to ask him about those days, not in any accusatory sense, but simply to get a villager's view of those turbulent times. When I asked, however, why the peasants cooperated, Shao merely said that they learned, "through education, the strength of cooperation."

Planned, mutual aid had brought members of the commune a life they could not have hoped for before Liberation, Shao said.

"The average family's income has increased three times since 1957, going from 110 yuan ($55) a year to 344 yuan ($172). Seven per cent of this is put back into the commune welfare fund. Food is provided free and each family has its own small private plot for vegetables and chickens."

Shao said he had no schooling. Less than 5 per cent of the children went to school before Liberation, and then only in the winter months when little farm work could be done.

"Now, 91 per cent of all the children go to school," said Shao. "There are fifty primary schools with 8,600 pupils, one high school with 600 and an agricultural college with 104 students."

These figures, although a great step forward in rural education, nevertheless indicate that only one in ten country children attend full-time school after the age of twelve. Night classes and after-work study groups supplement and extend the educational process into the late teens.

The commune also boasted fifty small health stations, eight clinics and one hospital. Patients for major surgery were sent to Canton.

41

Not only were social conditions on the upswing, said Shao, but also the yield of the commune's two main crops—rice and peanuts.

"As for pigs, in 1957 we had only 9,700. Now we have 42,630. Also, seven years ago we had only 126,000 poultry. Now we have 356,000."

Statistics such as these—as much as part of today's China scene as black braids and red banners—raise a problem. There is no conceivable way of verifying them: the alternatives are simply to accept or reject them. On the whole, Western writers seem to regard them as penny peepholes into the inner sanctum of the Chinese economy, but, repeatedly, it was my impression that the Chinese, no matter how religiously they quote them, regard them as a progressive novelty, not to be taken too seriously. As another example of this, Edgar Snow in his book, *The Other Side of the River*, quotes Wu Chen, vice-minister of agriculture, as indicating a taxable grain crop of 200 million tons for 1958, a figure which Yung Lung-kuei, then with the bureau of statistics, set "slightly" lower. Now, seven years later, when I interviewed Yung in Peking, he reports a "record" increase in grain output in 1964 to 200 million tons.

By now it had stopped raining: the sun filtered through to the flagstoned courtyard. I heard Shao conclude his talk with something I was to hear countless times:

"We must be diligent to keep up with advances and patient to help the backward."

We strolled outside to the cluster of buildings which, in every commune, are the center from which all official activity springs. The basketball court was inches under water. Newly planted saplings sagged around the recreation center's soggy fringes.

We passed a one-room nursery with its open door, windows on one side only. It was shadowy inside: there were none of the duck, bear and drum motifs of the nursery in almost any other land. Nor were there blackboards, desks, books, toys or crayons. Just wall benches and some sheets of colored paper which the children were manipulating into shapes. There were about twenty of them, three years and younger, and all were plump and warmly wrapped in padded cotton jackets and corduroy pants. They sang for us and their voices, vigorous and happy, filled the yard. By Western standards, it wasn't much of a nursery; but this wasn't the West, this was China, where in former years a quarter of these children might already have died from starvation; for the rest it would have been a long, thirty-year process. By this yardstick, the children's nursery was wonderful!

Then we drove through the mud, past endless rice paddies, past an irrigation canal built by 8,000 peasants in two months (we were told), and on to the hospital. It was a one-level building, white-washed and about the size of two modest ranch-style homes. It looked out over miles of rice paddies onto distant mountains. Inside, the high ceilings, the concrete block floors, the large and empty waiting room in the front lobby, lent the building a disconsolate air. Off the main corridor were small, bleak examination rooms with handmade wooden chairs and examination tables of plain wood boards. It took little imagination to see, however, that the hospital's importance did not derive either from the building standards or even from the care given: it derived rather from the mere fact that it was *there*—that the polemics of the party could deliver the goods! Now, when the body was hurt or broken, there was someone to turn to, some place to go for help. The psychological effects of this can hardly be overestimated among people who, over the centuries, led the way among the most downtrodden, starved and oppressed races on the face of the earth.

The hospital director, Dr. Fu An, unwittingly provided a

little international touch when he explained why the waiting room was empty.

"It's because it's Sunday," he explained through an interpreter. "There are many workers who choose this day for their holiday."

Apparently, as in the Western world, the aches and pains of life are more easily borne on a weekend than on a weekday!

Dr. Fu, a short, stocky man with a knee-length white coat over gray workclothes, took us to a room and continued his examination of a little boy with measles. The lad's mother sat in the corner, looking anxious.

"I have told her that the boy should stay with us for a few days," he said through the interpreter, but smiling a little at the mother's anxiety. "It's still a little strange for them. In the days before Liberation they would keep the children at home: there wasn't anywhere for them to go. Then they would all get sick. Sometimes, they would die with simple childhood diseases."

Dr. Fu, a graduate of the Red Cross Hospital in Canton, was a physician of traditional Chinese medicine. He said he used herbs and acapuncture as well as some modern medications and massage. Acapuncture is a technique for "stimulating" key nerve centers by insertion of a steel needle: it is used mainly for the relief of pain connected with motor and digestive disorders. Dr. Fu showed me his needles: the longest silver sliver was about four inches and the smallest perhaps half an inch. Chinese doctors study for six years, three of which are spent in residence. Possibly because of the use of acapuncture, great emphasis is placed on neurology.

Dr. Fu said an average of 100 patients came in during a week, that there was no compulsory tuberculosis program, but there was a birth-control program.

"It's more than 90 per cent successful," he said. He said the women use a ring. There was no pill available yet. (Production of a birth-control pill, with plans for mass distribution, was announced a few days before I left China. This is a change in official policy. For years the Peking government denied the necessity of controlling China's population, perhaps feeling it conflicted with that country's basic policy that its people are her final and ultimate strength.)

We were walking toward the commune's small hydroelectric plant when a revealing incident occurred.

I have always felt uncomfortable with the tourist habit of arbitrarily poking a camera in someone's face and taking a picture of him, particularly when his circumstances might be humiliating, or, as is often the case in the Orient, where many people still believe that taking a picture of them can somehow capture their soul. On this occasion, I had taken no shots because of rain. Now I looked into my camera out over the rice paddies, the sun reflected in the orderly rivulets: just then a peasant, a load strung on his bamboo pole, a wide coolie hat on his head, walked into camera range. I took his picture.

Within moments, Li Tieh-fei, the interpreter, was at my elbow, speaking softly but leaving no doubt as to the firmness of his message.

"Yu says it would be a pity to waste the film. Please do not take any films without asking the person's permission. There have been incidents where our people have asked visitors to expose a roll. This is their right. We would have to comply with such a request."

It didn't rest there. The following day, seated next to Yu in a bus, it was explained to me, carefully, patiently, that "the Chinese have a great sense of human dignity."

I didn't see one incident—even when wandering around alone—that contradicted Yu's claim. If I gave up my seat on a crowded bus to a working mother, struggling onto the bus with her toddlers after picking them up at the nursery, she took my seat unhesitatingly with a smile; if I stood for an old man, he took my seat with grave and quiet approval; if the restaurant maître d' accompanied us from the dining room to our bus, it was a gesture of courtesy untainted with waist-bowing obsequiousness; and, if a chance subject didn't want his or her picture taken, that person would hold up a hand in firm, brook-no-nonsense refusal.

After visiting the small hydroelectric station, which was fed by the waters of the peasant-built canal, we went through the dirt-floored wooden sheds in which all the repair work, and even some of the tools, are made for the commune.

It was in one of these workshops that I perceived for the first time the true character and extent of the Chinese revolution. It has struck at the hearts and minds of the lowliest peasant and elicited a response. I could not say whether it is a "Communist" revolution or not in the sense that I had no way of determining how much these peasants truly understand Marxist-Leninist principles. But it is a revolution, the authenticity of which is reflected not only in the farmyard toolshed, but in the numbers of buyers from scores of countries visiting China, for the first time in her history, for the sole purpose of purchasing her industrial products.

Looking around this commune workshop, whose austerity mocked the widely held notion that tourists are shown only dainty lantern-slide scenes or examples of vast progress, I saw rural China in a microcosm. With all the sweat of body and mind that the peasant can muster, he is heaving himself forward into the new society. One of the workers showed me a harrow he had made. He stood by it lovingly—a young man in his middle twenties—and earnestly watched my face as I peered at the odd metal scraps, some rusted, which he had welded together piece by piece to make his harrow. He had never seen a factory-built harrow, but someone had shown him a picture cut from a book.

Everywhere I went I was to see this groping, never-flagging

search for a better way to do things. Everywhere there is a spirit of research and innovation. In the communes, no matter how poor, there were one or two experimental plots for the growing of more and better quality grain; in the adjacent agricultural buildings there would be projects, involving two or three laboratory workers, aimed at improving the success rates of artificial insemination of pigs and cows, or of ridding the peanut crop of a small blight. The experience of "veteran peasants" and their ideas of how things should be done seemed to receive the same consideration as the views of laboratory workers with a university training. Together they work side by side, a talent duet personifying the oft-repeated admonition, theory must be combined with practice!

As for this worker's harrow, perhaps it would break up on stony ground: no matter, he would try again, and try harder.

The methods used in this workshop were a blend of the primitive and the progressive. The tool-making lathes were powered by the nearby hydroelectric plant—"We put in all the automatic belts ourselves," said Shao—but for all the repair, work furnaces and sledge hammers were going full swing. The smelting of the cast iron was done in little raised black clay mounds on a sloping dirt floor.

"Look at that!" cried Jack Clark, the seventy-nine-year-old retired Australian engineer. "That's just how I started out over fifty years ago! Here, give me a swing with that hammer, mate."

Jack took the sledge hammer and pounded the red-hot steel. He was in his element.

"Never thought I'd be swinging my hammer in China," he said, laughing.

I noticed there were no safety rails, not even on the circular saw, which was most inadequately lit with a single naked light-bulb. Later, however, visiting city factories, I noticed ample safety precautions around the machinery, and all buildings under construction had fenced-in safety walks. There was no evidence to support the notion that the Chinese are indifferent to, or careless about, human life.

I lingered at the door before I left, trying to visualize the shop as it would be twenty years from now. What would the revolution, born perhaps of both pressure and persuasion but coming to maturity now with an exploding force, bring within those years?

As I walked back to the bus I could see some peasants bent over the fields. For millions, life in China's new society goes on to all intents and purposes as it always has; up with the sun and down to the fields and then shiver or sweat until day is done. But there are differences—food at the end of the day, enough blankets on the bed, a school for one's children, a hospital in time of sickness. Life is primitive on the East Flower Commune of Canton, but, for its members, it has never been better. Their hope for even a brighter future seemed to me to have a most realistic foundation.

5

If you like to have

your head rubbed, a visit to a hairdresser or barber in China is a positive treat—a thoroughly decadent, pre-Liberation experience!

The equipment might be pathetically inadequate—the hair dryers in particular look like relics from some torture chamber—but what the hairdressers lack in material aid they more than compensate for in loving care. The results are surprisingly good.

With two hours free before our departure from Canton to Peking, I told Chin I wanted to have my hair washed.

"Yes, yes," said Chin, chirpy as always. "I will take you." He led me down to the second floor of the hotel and along a broad and ill-lit corridor. There was no sign to indicate the barber-hairdresser shop.

Equipment inside the large room looked like the rest of the city, gray and yellow with age. But it was clean, as is everything and everyone in China. To my slight dismay, there was a handsome Chinese youth in the barber chair next to mine. He was having his hair clipped. We cast covert glances at each other as I waited my turn. In one corner I could see an old dryer awaiting its next victim.

The barber didn't know a word of English. Chin told him I wanted my hair washed and set.

"It will cost 95 cents," he said and, with a brusque laugh, was on his way. About 40 U.S. cents!

The barber was tall, thin, and by now worried. I sat upright in the old brown leather barber chair as he poured a half bottle of some soapy mix over my head. The nails of his right hand were an inch long; his left hand was clipped neatly. The shampoo, all done as I sat there, took one half-hour: when the suds got too thick he lifted them off my hair with his fingers and started all over again. Content at last that my head was clean, he flipped the old barber chair back, my legs shot up and my head went into a bowl.

I wondered how many Chinese gentlemen were waiting for a trim and catching the entire show. I opened one wary eye but the only other person in the room was a pretty young mother sitting in the other chair with a boy of about two in her lap. Later, from the wails of the child and the laughter of the mother, I learned it was to be the lad's first haircut.

The rest of the appointment was essentially the same as in an American beauty shop—with the exception of the barber wanting to oil my hair down. He used large rollers and when the hair was finally dry, brushed it for fifteen minutes, pressing the waves in with his fingers, rather than glueing it down with spray.

I really regretted not being able to tip him but all tipping is forbidden in China. This rule makes for very good human and tourist relations. There is none of the fumbling for small change, the delighted or sullen reactions as you under- or over-tip in foreign currency. It is all part of the program of weeding out class distinctions. If you really need help with your bags going into a hotel, someone will turn up to give you a hand. But if you look physically healthy, are neither very old nor very young, you normally carry your own bags, or at least assist the bellboy in hauling the heavy stuff. If the bellboy then holds out his hand, it's to shake yours and wish you farewell.

Upstairs, I returned to my room. My luggage was packed ready to go. Within seconds Yu, the Communist party official, was at my door, making "Shoo shoo" gestures with his hands, telling me to hurry. Everyone else was in the bus. I peeked from my window and felt relieved to see some patches of blue in the overcast sky.

Before I left the United States, aware that I would be making some long airplane flights in China, I had tried to find out something about the safety record of the Chinese aircraft services but had been able to determine nothing. Soon I would be finding out firsthand!

We drove to the yellow, stucco-faced airport about thirty miles out of the city. The rain had stopped; the long straight asphalt roads, newly built, neatly lined with trees, carried a traffic of donkey-drawn carts filled with market produce. The wheels of these vehicles are often discarded truck tires. Some of the produce was being taken to market in carts drawn by women who, with a broad strap over one shoulder, pulled and strained like beasts of burden.

These women were to be seen everywhere in the areas adjoining the six cities I visited—short, needle-thin frames, the legacy of centuries of malnutrition, sometimes with a gold-filled front tooth, their brown child-like feet bare in thong sandals, their loose gray slacks and jackets flopping. Hauling, pushing, shoving, dissipating their energy and their lives on methods 2,000 years old, they haul out sand by the bucketful on construction projects, push wheelbarrows of bricks, are harnessed like oxen to a plough in the field. One can be seen on every country bypass going along at a breathless trot, sandals flapping, bundles of produce or sticks balanced at each end of the bamboo pole across her shoulders.

What difference could communism have made to the humdrum details of their daily lives, I wondered? Well, if it were just the fulfilled promise of some food each day, of a place to go and bear one's young, of somewhere to go and die in dignity, it was an improvement. The greatest contribution of communism, however, could well have been the removal of the specter of the landlord money-lender with all the fears and superstitions that they could conjure. Certainly, the Communist party had replaced this specter. But, authoritarian as it probably is in the disposition of people's labors, everything that I saw indicated a sincere and consistent attempt to invest the lowliest person with a sense of dignity and value, particularly with regard to his labors. The Chinese masses have always sweated through life in ways identical with those visible through the window of the bus. I doubt, however, that these poor women had ever been told before communism came, that their labors, as well as themselves, are of worth and value. Nor do I have any doubt that these women are now using a new vocabulary, words that their female ancestors back through the centuries had rarely spoken —the vocabulary of the person who has a glimpse of hope and a modicum of dignity as opposed to the drudge whose lifelong milieu is despair.

Such hopes are probably based more on the visible changes in the rural areas—such as finding the landlord abolished, hearing his legendary callousness systematically deplored at political meetings, seeing the communes formed —than by the official edicts giving women equal rights that came out of Peking following Liberation. Until then, a woman could not inherit property; furthermore, she was the "property" of her husband. She had no legal rights: he could do with her as he wished. If she worked—if she was fortunate enough to find work—she received smaller wages, and it was not unusual for her to be given less food within the family accordingly.

Now Chinese women receive equal pay for equal work and the money is paid directly to them. They are also entitled to fifty-six days of paid maternity leave each year.

None of the property rights would be of much value to these women, I thought, as the bus sped along. Nor would the die-hard peasant farmers have changed their marital attitudes overnight. But the Communists have given these women, after centuries of being treated as animals, legal recourse, some sense of security and some glimpse of hope for their children's future.

We had been told we would be leaving Canton airport at 3:30, but at 4 we were still sitting around the large modern lobby with its plastic lounges, colorful chrome table and chairs, souvenir shop—all presided over by a white plaster bust of Chairman Mao Tse-tung. After our fifth cup of green tea we were told we would be having dinner there. As we left for the adjoining dining room, I noticed a British Viscount aircraft ready to take off.

By 5:30, dinner was over and we were ready to go. It was still light and a slight drizzle did little to cut down visibility. Again, I wondered about the maintenance and upkeep of aircraft within China, not to mention pilot skill.

There were no seat numbers given; first on, first served, and every seat was occupied. For a moment, with people standing bewildered in the aircraft's jam-packed corridor, it appeared that too many tickets had been sold. At last, everyone was seated. I was on the right side of the aircraft in a row of three seats. There were two seats on the other side.

Somewhat to my surprise, the interior of the aircraft was furnished exactly the same as aircraft in commercial use in any major city of the world. The floor was carpeted, the cur-

53

tains had some sort of fancy metallic thread, and the walls were covered in a quiet, vaguely futuristic design.

At no time, nor in any other plane, did I see any of the crew other than the stewardesses. These little girls, with short hair and navy jacket and slacks and matching navy beret, gave the usual safety instructions in both Chinese and English. They made no mention of oxygen masks, however. Expressing the hope that we would enjoy the flight, they pointed out that it was a government regulation that no binoculars or cameras were to be used in flight. There were no restrictions, however, while we were on the ground, either in the aircraft or around the airport.

I buckled on my seat belt and looked around at the other passengers.

The group on this plane was typical of my fellow passengers on all aircraft—a sprinkling of Communist officials in their quality gray semiofficial suits; three or four young women in their early twenties or even younger, wearing waist-length black braids and navy slacks and jackets of denim; half a dozen Japanese businessmen; some British buyers; two Australian salesmen; a handful of middle-aged Chinese men, perhaps engineers or factory managers. With the exception of the party officials, the Chinese looked like members of the laboring worker class. It comes as a shock to realize that's the only class there is! Who else could be riding the aircraft? They might be college professors or doctors or students going off on a special project, but they are still workers and they dress like it—if decidedly important workers, since they were flying to Peking rather than doing the two-day, two-night train trip. One feature was the absence of the very old and the very young.

Interpreter Li Tieh-fei sat next to me, and a rosy-cheeked young girl with braids and slacks sat next to him.

The plane taxied around for take-off.

"Li," I asked, "how good are Chinese pilots?"

"The best in the world," he said very earnestly. He added that they won't fly in a rain-storm, and I wondered if that was the reason for our delay.

The take-off was smooth and quick—no lining up for your turn as in the United States. In fact, we appeared to be the only aircraft then on the field. (Only twice, the entire time I was in China, did I hear the whump of a jet streaking overhead.)

Then we were up and on our way to Peking, a five-hour flight with an hour stopover to let off and pick up passengers in Shanghai.

Fiddling around in my flight bag, I produced a bottle of *mao tai*, a colorless liqueur with a kick like a mule. Charles Roberts, one of the Australians on the tour, had bought it during our dinner at Canton airport to celebrate our flight to Peking.

I held up the stone bottle and asked:

"What am I going to do with this?"

"I suggest, Mrs. Hobbs, that you put it away—immediately," Li said. I looked at him: his face was as stony as the bottle.

This was my first, but not last, encounter with current Chinese attitudes toward anything to do with *la dolce vita*. In my astonishment at what was essentially a reprimand, I put the bottle away—just in time to look back down the corridor toward the end of the plane and see Communist official Yu take off his pants! Taking his good time, he pulled down a package and took out a pair of rust-colored hand-knitted longjohns and slipped them over the white woolen longjohns he already had on. I grinned—and he grinned back, not one whit disconcerted.

The temperature steadily dropped as we went north. The Westerners read, the Chinese dozed. Many of the Westerners still carried with them light reading—paperbacks and glossy magazines—brought with them from Hong Kong; nothing like this is available in China. The only reading material available is approved literature, such as plays and stories with a socialist message, political tomes, propaganda pamphlets, and newspapers: nothing whose value is sheer entertainment. Soon one of the hostesses was passing out coffee or tea with a box of mixed Chinese cookies and delicacies. I offered one to Li: he was a pale lime green, which I came to recognize as his usual flight pallor.

He shuddered and gently pushed the delicacies away. That had been my reaction when I saw them too, as they looked rather cold and congealed, but his reasons for refusal were different.

"Are you scared of flying?" I asked.

"Of course not." He laughed thinly and tapped his forehead. "Just a headache."

It was 11 p.m. before we touched down at Shanghai. Flights to Peking from Canton stop either there or at Wuhan for passengers. We were almost on it before the city could be seen: that blaze of light that glows in the sky for miles before an American metropolis is sighted was absent. There were a few lights, but it could have been some island in the South Pacific from the air.

We were taken by bus from the plane to a nearby hangar which had been converted into a lounge. Tea was served. We ran into an English woman of about fifty, a secretary who, fed up with London's fog, had decided to see the world. She had entered China through Hong Kong after a mere five days' wait for a visa. There was a Canadian couple there, too, waiting for the flight to Peking. He was a farmer; they were vacationing. Like most of the foreigners we met in China, we were to run into them time and time again at airports, railway stations and at different resorts. With only nine cities in China "open" to the tourist and with limited hotel facilities and passenger flights, chance encounters were almost inevitable. When I asked later why only nine cities were open, I was told that few Chinese cities have hotel accommodations suitable for Westerners, but that more and more cities would be opened as hotels were constructed. People who had lived in China before Liberation, and who now reside in San Francisco, told me later that it is a fact that Westerners more or less had clung to east coast cities in former days precisely for this same reason. It is ironic that some of the travel restrictions arbitrarily imposed by the Communist regime were practiced voluntarily in earlier times.

We were off again, and now the temperature was decidedly low. Li took off his cashmere sweater and suggested I use it. I had not mentioned I was cold. His solicitous gesture was typical of the paternal attitude the interpreters and even Communist party officials seemed to have toward the visitor. Were such acts calculated to impress? I don't think so. There is a certain kind of solicitude and courtesy that are intuitive: no amount of teaching can impart this perception. Time and time again I noticed how gentle the Chinese were, one with another, no matter how abusive and crude the public name-calling of Peking's official statements.

Now we were to fasten our seat belts: soon our ears were popping. It was unbelievable: I was over Peking! It was 1 a.m. and we were filing out into a chill wind. An interpreter named Mrs. Chia, a woman in her late twenties or early thirties, was there to meet us and take us into the vast marble-floored terminal, where tea was served. She looked very tired, and I had no doubt that she had been waiting there while we dined in Canton waiting for the showers to pass.

It was home, too, for Yu, Li and Wang, but in Communist China that makes very little difference. All three were to stay with us at the Nationalities Hotel, despite the fact that the two married men had their wives and families in the outer suburbs. During our week there, however, they were given a day and night off.

Said Lois Carter, an Australian housewife in her early fifties:

"What a pity, Li, that you can't go home."

He said he lived too far out in the suburbs, that at that hour of night it would be absurd.

"But what a pity," Lois said. "Your wife might be waiting."

Said Li, with a smile but an edge of exasperation in his voice:

"Truly, I think my wife is quite capable of living a week or two without me."

It was an interesting illustration of a Western woman's traditional, sentimental concept of marriage and home life as compared to the new look in Chinese marriages. In my thirteen years as a journalist, however, spent working mainly with men, I know of many who would have envied Li—not his house, job, or life, but his freedom from domestic responsibility for a week or two while he fulfilled a specific job. Certainly, there were times when I thought that the women interpreters, despite their long hours, didn't have to shoulder half the responsibilities that are thrust onto the shoulders of the working mother here. Nurses for small children are easy to obtain, so are cooks. And as the state approves of women contributing what they can to the new society, these women are freed from what is perhaps the greatest single source of irritation for American working mothers—a nagging sense of guilt.

Now we were in the bus, a foam-cushioned plush affair with antimacassars on the head- and armrests. We sped through the deserted tree-lined country roads made sickly purple with mercury lights. And then—the capital!

6

To visit Peking is to
catch the past by its tail and to be pulled into a vision of the future.

The dimensions of Tien An Men (Heavenly Peace Gate) Square—it holds 800,000 persons—the size of the Great Hall of the People, the sky-grasping columns of the Museum of the Revolution, the width of the sweeping, tree-lined boulevards, these are part of the show-garden of the new society.

All were visible in one breath-taking glance when we tumbled out of the bus in the Tien An Men Square on the morning following our arrival in Peking.

But turn from looking to the south and look to the north of the square and then the full dimension of Peking's physical beauty is encompassed. The red and gold lacquered beauty of the past continues its opulent, independent existence, indifferent to the political gyrations of this or past centuries. In one sublime glance, the eyes fall on turquoise tiles, glazed and jewel-like; a moat, spanned by a marble bridge; pink, crenellated walls; gray bastions and lions; and underneath one's feet might be flagstones worn smooth through many centuries.

Yet, despite the impact of the past, this must be the least mummified of all the world's ancient cities. Modern buildings are all around, making no attempt to match the imperial extravagance of the old with their golden dragons and lavender tiles, but surpassing this extravagance in a lavishness of sheer bulk. The result is that the buildings of the past sit in incredible harmony with those of the present, almost as if the Chien Men Tower and the Tien An Men Gate, facing each other over the half-mile square, had been designed centuries ago to be flanked by the Hall of the People and the Museum of the Revolution.

It is likely that the size of the buildings which surround the square, the heart of Peking, and all the main arteries leading into this heart, were not determined by aesthetic considerations alone. Nor would it be accurate to interpret the city's massive splurge in mortar as an ostentatious attempt to impress the visitor while bolstering the spirits of the Pekingese. From what I saw in China, Peking appeared to be a visible expression of a deep and hidden reality. The size and grandeur of the concrete structures are reflections of the Chinese dream—an open display of that country's potential accomplishments, a "concrete" expression of what she can achieve.

That this dream is still some distance from accomplishment is apparent with a stroll along any boulevard.

There are very few automobiles. Every few minutes a cab or an official car flies by. In Peking, these are generally the Chinese built Red Flag or Phoenix design—a six-cylinder ninety horse power product—or the small Russian Zims. (In Canton and Shanghai, I had noticed a few vintage Buicks, Fords and Chryslers, and some British Vauxhalls and Humbers, but no Chinese products.)

It is a rare Peking resident, indeed, who travels by anything other than bus, pedicab or bicycle. There are no rickshaws. The clean red and white buses go by in a steady flow:

bus stops, identified with a large Roman numeral for the corresponding service, are staggered along the main boulevards for various destinations. The people line up without shoving. During the jam-packed rush hours transportation is doubled by hooking a motorless vehicle to the back of a regular bus.

Those with a load to carry take a pedicab: others go by bicycle. They move down the streets in never-ending streams, legs in navy sailcloth going rhythmically, pausing at the corners for the overhead traffic lights strung in the center of each crossroad. Here the traffic police have their own glass-enclosed booths and keep the traffic in line by means of a public address system. Alternately, they stand on the corner, neat with their red-belted white jackets, navy caps, and slacks, and give their orders and reprimands through a bullhorn.

Everyone lucky enough to own a bike rides it to work. Most job sites have free parking lots: otherwise it costs 2 cents a day to park (1 U.S. cent).

The housing in Peking is much the same as it has always been. Get off the vast boulevards with their thirteen-bulb, magnolia-shaped lamps and into the *hutungs*—the maze of small alleys that wind through the city—and you are back in the past. Flat gray walls like dingy cardboard run along the packed-dirt alleys. Stone entrances—sometimes emblazoned with a red banner exhorting greater effort by the workers—open into courtyards around which countless dwellings morosely face another century. The doors to the homes are wooden: in the winter they are covered with a heavy, padded screen to block out the icy winds. Bamboo sticks protrude from some windows. The jackets that we saw the residents wearing by the thousands were all padded with cotton, or sometimes worn sheepskin. Usually, this padding is removed and only the cotton exterior of the jacket is washed; but, come spring, the padding and the lambskin fillings are washed and

61

thrust out into the sun to dry. At night, heat is provided by charcoal braziers and then locked in the room by the padded screen over the door and thick translucent paper over the window. The floors are covered with reed mats. Some of the homes I saw had electricity and running water. Others did not. The real comforter against the snow of winter and the chill blasts of Peking's spring is the *kang*, the broad, 7-foot-long bed made of bricks and mud, on which the little children play during the day and the family sleeps at night. The *kang* is heated by a fire stocked on the outside: the hot air enters from the side of the house flowing directly under the bed. (In the rural areas I noticed that the *kangs* were heated with hot air flowing from the cooking stove.)

There has been one remarkable change over the past few years, however. These humble shelters are no longer the source of epidemics. Courtyards have been swept clean until they are rock-hard. Not a fragment of litter can be seen. Street cleaners walk through the alleys in the morning sprinkling water on the dust. Human excrement, used as a fertilizer in agriculture, is collected daily and the air is pure. (The widespread use of excrement in China's rural areas does more than a little to dissipate the pleasures of rustic scenery on a warm day.)

On the outskirts of Peking—and in Canton and Shanghai —large housing projects in the form of five- to eight-story complexes are spreading into what was undoubtedly countryside just months ago. All these projects have steam heat, butane gas, electricity, running water and shopping centers. None have elevators. Many had box-like outside balconies and looked depressingly like the type of mass public housing going up everywhere in the world. I gained the impression that it is younger people who are moved into this housing. Whether this is true or not, it appeared obvious that even with one family to a room most of China's city dwellers over forty will be deceased before there is room for them in the new projects.

Chia told us that the construction of home units in Peking had risen 285 per cent over the past ten years compared to a similar period in pre-Liberation days. By the number of apartment buildings that I saw under construction, I would say that the government is providing the people with a sufficiently increasing number of new apartments to maintain a slim hope that they might one day move into one. It isn't a stream, just a steady trickle, as if the government is concerned but cannot jeopardize the gains it has made elsewhere to splurge on nonproductive investments such as housing. I saw one high-rise apartment project outside Peking—a series of five buildings—partially completed and with no sign of any activity. This was on a weekday and when I asked Chia where the workmen were, I was told it was their holiday. The project looked to me as if it hadn't been worked on for some time: it had a desolate air. There was no equipment of any sort to be seen anywhere, not even the small cement mixers which they use and which, I noticed, are left on construction jobs overnight.

If the people of Peking are oppressed by the state of their housing they don't look it. Strolling along the boulevards, wandering alone through the *hutungs,* I was struck by the general demeanor of dignity and self-confidence. Despite the fact that there are now seven million people in and around Peking—four million in the city proper—and despite the fact that all but the old or young are employed in one project or another, the streets are never crowded to the point where one is pushed off the sidewalk. Lack of mobility and staggered days off are undoubtedly contributing reasons.

Are the people happy? Frankly, I don't know any more than I would know whether a random crowd in the streets of

London, New York or Los Angeles were happy. They seemed to be leading purposeful and organized lives; for the mass of the people this probably makes for contentment. There was no indication of individual wealth nor any of individual want. Without exception, everyone appeared warmly, cleanly dressed. On cold days the children wore caps and ear muffs with their quilted coats and pants. Scores of little stores peddling candied fruits and nuts did a thriving business. Larger fresh fruit stores, with their produce neatly displayed, were generally crowded. These stores lend a feeling that the city hadn't been stripped to the bone of little luxuries and treats. The ease with which people smiled, the speed with which they enjoyed a joke, appeared to indicate a basic contentment.

One night I took a bus and went to the downtown shopping area looking for Liu Li Chang, the famous street of antique shops. I had no map but had passed it earlier in the day and knew only the general direction. I stopped a score of Chinese asking, with various intonations, Liu Li Chang? while at the same time pointing toward the area in which the street lay. Some laughed at me in total bewilderment but stood by trying to help, a couple smiled and cocked their ear toward me while I repeated the words, some shook their heads and walked on, but no one shied back in fear of getting mixed up with a foreigner; no one hurried away from me without genuinely trying to help.

What is the attitude of the Chinese toward the stranger? It is invariably one of friendship, although the degree varies from city to city, presumably depending on how familiar foreigners have become in different cities. For instance, we were among the first Westerners to visit Wusih, a beautiful lake-area resort only recently opened to tourist groups. We were treated there as if we had come from another planet: the people gathered in crowds to stare solemnly. There was nothing hostile about it, but when I remarked to Li that they didn't appear too friendly and no one smiled, he said with a little edge of irritation, as if the snap cultural judgments of Westerners became at times abrasive:

"Have you ever thought that these people simply might be shy?"

The one firm characteristic in all cities was the lack of overt dislike or hostility. There might have been a flat refusal to be photographed, a turning of the back to the camera, a snatching of a child out of camera range by a stern-faced older woman, but these were the exceptions.

In Peking, the people are certainly more accustomed to foreigners than in towns such as Wusih. Yet, as we left the plush Nationalities Hotel in Peking each day to ride our equally plush bus, pedestrians would stop for a moment to look, and fathers out wheeling their babies in homemade wooden prams would cross the hotel's forecourt to get a better look. On the bus and in the stores, most of the people were politely indifferent—or they assumed this pose.

Toward one another, there was an easy, familiar respect. They are very careful not to shove or hustle each other. Like people everywhere, I noticed some bus passengers would give up their seats to the aged or mothers with young children, and some wouldn't. I did notice, however, that none of the jaunty young girls who comprised Peking's bus conductor force hesitate to haul one of the reluctant out of his seat if she thinks someone else should take priority. When this happened, there was never any back talk. The government runs constant campaigns to improve the people's manners, already among the most elegant in the world. This quality of "elegance" is a simple, graceful serenity, a certain poise, that the most humbly-situated Chinese seems to possess. The manners on which the government is now insisting aren't based on traditional upper-class mores—although they apparently do not intrude on them—but on a widening of social consciousness, the developing of a sense of responsibility of one citizen for another. This sense of community is a striking feature of today's China—a passerby picking up the parked but fallen bicycle of a stranger and setting it gently back against a post; women shoppers peering at vegetables and fruits for quality and not bruising them for the next customer; children stopping a game without being asked to let an aged person through. Such sights are so common that the tourist soon begins to take them for granted.

Toward the white-jacketed traffic police, shouting their orders through a megaphone or from a raised booth on the sidewalk, there is an attitude of surprising indifference. The pedicab driver with a load, the late student on his bicycle, the mother hurrying home, will all risk a bawling-out to cross against the traffic if it suits their purpose.

How do the Chinese dress? When I was there it was spring and I didn't see one woman in a dress anywhere. However, I was assured by an irate translator when I remarked about this, that the women wear nothing but dresses during the summer; further, shorts are popular among the girls. Bolts of bright cotton in the stores indicated that the women do bloom in summer. Certainly, their sense of style and fashion hibernates during the winter. Like the men, they wear quilted sailcloth jackets and pants in either navy or some shade of gray.

As they wear no cosmetics whatsoever, nor any jewelry, the result is remarkably de-sexing by Western standards. It has proved no problem to Chinese men, however, if one is to judge by the number of young fathers proudly hauling their children off to the park.

Many writers speak of the "conformity" of Chinese dressing, the inference being that it is a reflection or proof of the "conformity" of the Chinese mind. It was my impression that the Chinese dress as warmly and as cheaply as their economy permits them. If navy blue sailcloth or gray cotton is "conforming," it is certainly not more so than a brown or gray flannel suit, nor the white cotton dhotis that the Indians wear by the millions.

I did notice that the children wore a wide range of styles and a variety of colors and cloths. Most of them wore short little pinafore jackets and corduroy pants. Among primary and high school students, floral quilted jackets, bright green sweaters, burgundy slacks, gave every indication of incipient fashion consciousness.

The children were always well-dressed and with a greater degree of individuality than their parents, suggesting that, if there were a few extra yuan for a little touch of luxury in dress, it would go on the children.

The pants that the toddlers wear all have a back patch that can be let down for toilet purposes. They don't wear diapers or underpants, and one of the grave omissions of my trip was my failure to find out how they are toilet-trained. Perhaps the parents constantly resort to the little porcelain pots scattered along the main streets and in the park.

In any case one of the most charming sights in China is a very common one—a toddler, muffled from head to toe asleep on his dad's shoulder, a plump rear end exposed to the wind and the world. On a half-dozen occasions I was on the verge of taking a picture but by now I was so sensitive about Chinese dignity that I didn't dare!

There are several large department stores in Peking. They are well-stocked with most of the necessities of daily living and a few of the smaller luxuries such as fine soaps and perfumed hair oil. The counters containing sporting goods, such as table tennis sets, handball bats, rubber-coated hardballs, could have been anywhere in the world. Near the extremely popular sports section, always placed toward the back of the ground floor of the stores I saw, was a large section for bicycles, which ranged in price from 150 to 200 yuan (about $75–$100).

Most of the stores are two, or at the most three, stories, and the interior is plain and simple, rather like the department stores were when I was a child—linoleum and no carpeting; broad stairways, no elevators; glass counters, trimmed in dark veneered wood, with blouses and slacks neatly folded in stacks.

There were no change rooms to try clothes on: no need to, as an ample looseness, particularly across the beam, is a characteristic of Chinese dressing.

I tried to buy a set of navy blue cotton workclothes at Peking's largest store. This comprised a thin cotton top with a high collar and "frogs" closing the jacket on a diagonal line.

Both men and women worked behind the counter and I waited my turn. Finally, quite businesslike, a bespectacled fortyish salesman raised his eyebrows at me and I pointed at the workpants, which both men and women bought identically. He looked at me and took out a pair that my whole family could have gotten into. I gesticulated and asked for a smaller size. He raised his hand in a "stop" sign, made scrubbing motions, and then held his hands together to indicate the pants would shrink—to half size by his estimate. They are tied by a cord, just like pajama pants, and he also pulled this in to indicate a way of getting a better "fit." I continued to protest and he dug out another pair.

No one took much notice of me as I stood by the counter and held them up against my waist; one young girl giggled. All set on the purchase, I took my purchase slip to the cashier's glassed-in booth. But I had forgotten about the cotton ration. Without any coupons, I had no choice but to return the slacks to the salesman. I left him untangling the mess on his abacus.

The abacus, by the way, is still in universal use. Its click,

click, click as the round, brown spools are flicked into position, accompany every money transaction—even the adding of one yuan to another yuan!

Once I remarked on the fact that this addition—one and one—required eight or ten hand movements. I was told the clerk was "rechecking for accuracy."

There are "Friendship Stores" in all major cities. Here the tourist can buy goods at half price; there is also a wider range of products than is obtainable at the downtown department stores. For instance, at a store used by the people there might be one or two bolts of silk yardage on sale; the tourist in the Friendship Stores could choose from a dozen bolts. Conversely, there will be scores of bolts of bright, patterned cotton—apparently ready for spring—offered in the ordinary stores but there was none in the Friendship Stores, as it is a rationed item. Both stores offered wool yardage. In the ordinary stores there was no jewelry on sale (although there were ceramic and pottery goods); the Friendship Stores, on the other hand, had a wide and excellent selection of turquoise and jade jewelry and *objets d'art* at world market, not cheap, prices.

I found the ceramics, pottery and artwork to be of a consistently lower standard than that of the turquoise and jade work. Shopping one afternoon on Liu Li Chang, I mentioned this discrepancy to a genial shopkeeper, a man in his middle fifties, who spoke very good English. He said that most tourists find ceramic or pottery work too cumbersome to take with them, so the fine artwork was all exported commercially, the tourist buying easily portable objects, such as jade figures and turquoise necklaces. The English of this shopkeeper was so good I wondered if he were the former owner. Furthermore, he actually tried to sell his products, as if he were a salesman from way back. This was in contrast to most shopkeepers who, while being helpful and polite, are basically indifferent as to whether you buy or not; it makes no difference to them. The money is picked up at week's end and given to the government anyway!

I tried to find out details of this but without success. Incredible though it might seem, the cities of China are now divided up into districts, blocks and then streets. Each street has its own committee. This committee is responsible for all that goes on in the street designated as being under its control. It appoints the streetcleaners, acts as an employment agency for domestic help. I did not think to ask if it is responsible for picking up cash receipts from each shop and stall weekly. However, in every part of the city the money is collected and taken to a central office. Another official is responsible for checking the stock, another for authorizing new orders and stock replacements.

However plainly the Chinese are living, it didn't extend to the Nationalities Hotel where our group stayed. My double room was furnished with two lounge chairs separated by a coffee table, a desk and hard chair. The floor was carpeted and the room steam-heated. The heavy draperies worked on a drawstring and there were light muslin panels for daytime use. The old-fashioned wire screens could be easily removed for picture-taking of the city; the Chinese, unused to such technical adaptations, must have done a lot of puzzling when, day after day, they found the screens on the floor in my room and, day after day, reinserted them!

Wherever I stayed, I had a private telephone and tiled bathroom. The black phone was identical to the American cradle type and my only complaint about the bathrooms was that they were inadequately lit. This complaint springs from the fact that I had to put on my make-up in the bathroom, since mirrors were very rarely provided in the bedrooms.

This is just part of the miscellany of facts and impressions gained during my week-long stay in Peking.

When I remember Peking, however, these are not the things that immediately spring to mind. They were just the background against which an intriguing—and at times downright worrying—sequence of events was to get under way, all of them based on my illegal entry. Increasingly, I found myself wondering what the Chinese would do if they, for any slight purpose, ran a cross check on my visa application and turned up the fact that I was a reporter for the most conservative chain of newspapers in the United States. The virulence of the anti-American propaganda that now faced me at every turn offered no consolation whatsoever.

7

The moon came out,

as serene as ever, on the evening of May Day.

Despite the frosty air and light drizzle, the crowds came out in force, pouring down the boulevards into Tien An Men Square. There was nothing for the crowds to do but the air was crisp with expectation.

The city was now ablaze with light. Every main building, traced with thousands of yellow bulbs, was visible in outline. The city's centuries dropped away in the darkness as buildings such as the Great Hall of the People and the centuries old Ch'ien Men Tower displayed their lights in equal importance.

May Day is one of the two great festive days in China. The other is October 1. Both days are the focal point of the "social season" for visiting dignitaries from all over the world. Now, 5,000 of them were arriving for the official banquet at the Great Hall: the entrance was floodlit as large black shining limousines, which I had not seen in use before, deposited their shimmering and exotic guests mainly from African and East European nations. A handful of tense, young soldiers were scattered along the street, but the crowd of citizens, hands in their rough blue suits and silent, merely wanted to look.

Luxingshe had arranged a Peking duck dinner for those who fell into the foreign but nondignitary category. At 7 p.m., a little gussied up for the occasion (I wore gloves, only to be told by one of the Australian women that "the Chinese never wear gloves"), we drove in our bus to a downtown restaurant, where we were shown into an upstairs banquet hall used for gatherings of several hundred.

This was The Great Concentrated Morality Restaurant. The drab street entrance opened into a carpeted lobby with floor to ceiling mirrored walls on both sides: the wide staircase was also carpeted, but the actual eating hall was undecorated and utilitarian. Who cared about the furniture, however, as an army of cooks moved in from the back of the hall to march between the tables, smart in white with a French chef's cap and each bearing proudly Peking's internationally famous gastronomic fete, the golden Peking duck—the *canard lacqué*.

As they were borne away to be sliced, the toasting began, led by a tall, gray-haired Communist party official at the head table. This was my initiation into the fact that the Chinese might not approve of the unscheduled appearance of a bottle of *mai tai* on a plane, but at a formal ceremonial dinner they drink as if prohibition is to be imposed momentarily. There was one drink of that white and wicked liqueur, and before I could recover my breath, we were on our feet again for another. All over the hall, at round tables for eight, the toasts were translated simultaneously into the various languages of the guests. After the fourth toast, I noticed the little old German ladies at the adjoining table were having difficulty getting to their feet and the Japanese at another table were beginning to laugh too loudly. Soon enough, I thought, someone will start singing, and before we were through the preparatory courses—cold dishes of ham slices, duck feet in

mustard sauce, 100-year eggs (some called them "rotten eggs")
and fried liver—a voice was raised in song.

Before the banquet had reached this stage of May Day
fervor, however, we were given an official speech of "welcome"
by the top official. It was a virulent attack on American policy
in North Viet Nam; some of the guests warmly applauded,
some didn't. Most of the Japanese, I noted, did not. We settled down finally to the serious business of eating—but not
before the official had come to each table and shared another
toast, tipping glasses personally.

"Where are you from?" he asked through a nearby translator.

Through a *mai tai* haze, I realized it would not be appropriate at all to say San Francisco, but I had to bite my tongue
to keep it back. Aware of the fact that I was standing with my
tongue between my teeth, I tried to cover my confusion by
pouring my *mai tai* into his empty glass. Superbly straight, he
bowed in my direction, downed it in one, and moved onto the
next table, where the plump German ladies made up for their
inability to rise by emitting little gusts of wild laughter.

But still, we weren't to eat. Now we had to toast one
another at the table. Led by Yu Shang-ven, our "own"
Communist party official, we quit drinking *mai tai* by un-
spoken mutual agreement and drank instead a sweet grape
wine. As the 100-year eggs got even older, Yu invited my
husband and children to come to China next time with me.

Finally, the sliced duck was brought to the table where we
ate it rolled in a special pancake, not unlike a tortilla, or in
soft rolls and dipped in a soya paste. It was followed by a soup
made of the bones. The instant it was finished we rose in Chinese style and went home. But not before I had asked if we
could go on to some sort of club or some place where we
could dance.

"I could dance all night," I said. "What about it, Li?"

"It is not healthy to dance all night," replied Li.

And that was that!

But the evening was not quite over. Earlier in the day I had walked downtown to the Peking Foreign Language bookstore and had purchased the beautifully illustrated edition of Rewi Alley's translation of *The Eighteen Laments* written by a woman named Tsai Wen-chi around the beginning of the third century.

Back at the Nationalities Hotel, I asked Yu Shang-ven to inscribe the date and place in Chinese in the book as a souvenir for me. He took the book, looked at it page by page, seemed highly suspicious of my request, which now made me groan inwardly, and then handed the book to translator Li. Said Li, stony-faced, passing on Yu's remark:

"You could have it seen to in Canton!"

The brusqueness of the refusal, after the evening's hospitality, floored me. I was both hurt and angry. A sense of hopelessness in trying to establish any normal, spontaneous relationship with the Chinese sent me to bed in gloom.

The sound of men marching and a thousand voices singing awoke me—at dawn. I got out of bed and from my window could see an endless stream of workers, red banners held high, moving out of the dawn to the center of town. The singing faded but the sound of softly shod feet moving on unpausing, intent, did not cease all day. There was no knowing how far these men had marched to reach Peking by daybreak.

I dressed and went to the front balcony. The sounds of the *Internationale* blared out of the loudspeakers along Chang An Boulevard. The sun was now rising. Over Tien An Men Square the huge crimson balloon lanterns were released, their red tails flying, to greet the day. The silk of the multi-colored banners flicked and swooped like bright-plumaged birds as a breeze sped across town.

The incident of the previous evening still rankled. I still

75

felt foolish, and when I turned to find Li Tieh-fei with his hand extended in a "good morning" handshake, I took it out of pragmatic desire not to mar the day with any further unpleasantness. But I had determined to be as cool as a Peking winter's morn from then on. But Yu Shang-ven had other ideas. He hustled out of his bedroom, opposite mine, and straight to my side, indicating to me that he wanted to talk. The three of us sat in the furnished lobby onto which the three elevators opened.

From the conversation that followed, I can only guess at what must have happened after I had gone to bed.

Nightly, after tourists go their separate ways, the interpreters and party officials gather in a hotel bedroom for a period that includes a summary of the day's events, a discussion of the next day's schedule, and a period of "self-criticism." This latter period, a thoroughly monastic idea, allows any member of the party either to be the humble recipient of criticism from others in his group or to "confess" errors made during the day—wrong attitudes adopted, and so on. These criticisms are based on what the ideal Marxist-Leninist man, freed of all interior and exterior class distinction, should act like.

But it doesn't stop there. These periods also include a discussion of the attitudes of the "guests." These nocturnal post-mortems were never admitted to by our officials; to my knowledge no one ever asked them directly. But they have been admitted to scores of other tourists; some officials make no secret of them. Their existence in our case was confirmed by our officials unwittingly touching on incidents or conversations that occurred when they were absent but one of the other officials was present. Once in a train, for instance, one of the Australians commented on the news that was being broadcast through our compartment's public-address system. Only one English-speaking interpreter heard his remark but the following day a non-English speaking party official mentioned the incident. The fact that any conversation of political importance is repeated creates an accumulating feeling of strain and uncertainty. One French journalist aptly described it as "a feeling of suffocation." I felt this acutely. The ultimate outcome is that the sensitive person, on his most integrated day, still feels he must watch himself.

To return to the incident of *The Eighteen Laments*, Yu either immediately realized something was up when I walked off in high dudgeon or he had been told. He apologized sincerely for what, he said, was a simple misunderstanding. He did not know what I wanted and he hoped that I would understand and not be angry about it.

Yu then added that he had come from an extremely poor peasant family. He had not moved in the world of books, in fact, he had not learned to read and write until he was nearly twenty. He had not before heard of the British custom of signing a book as a gesture of friendship or a souvenir, but now he understood and hoped I would, too.

It was an obvious explanation and quite likely the truthful one. However, his actions betrayed a disproportionate suspicion about something which he didn't understand immediately and for which he was totally unprepared.

With that out of the way, we shook hands and set out for the May Day festivities.

It was ten o'clock but the parks were already crowded. We left our bus in the square, now a moving sea of dark blue, and crossed the ancient moat into Peihai Park. Traditional Chinese music, like a hundred flutes, filled the air with a thin and delicate sound.

I joined a group of folk dancers: students, young factory workers, and members of the Liberation Army. They clapped and hopped without a trace of self-consciousness, but when they whirled around to find me as their partner, they invariably betrayed surprise. The young black-braided girls laughed and tried to help me with the steps, but the soldiers were embarrassed and shyly looked away. They were all well-built boys—it is an Occidental myth that Chinese men are short—and most of them were so light skinned that the dancing brought a bloom to their cheeks. They looked no older than teen-agers, their uniforms were clean but badly fitted and, like all the soldiers I saw in China, none of them carried any weapons of any sort. For all I know, they could have been generals. All officers in the Chinese army wear uniforms identical to privates', a small collar tab alone designating rank.

I had half-expected a military parade but there was not even a procession.

I commented on this to one of the four interpreters accompanying our group and was told there was no military parade even on National Day, October 1.

"The only armed marchers at that parade are the home militia," I was told. "We do not, as a peace loving nation, display arms."

This assertion appears to be true. Although pictures of highly organized "spontaneous" demonstrations against "U.S. Imperialism" appear with predictable regularity, I have not been able to obtain any pictures of displays of arms in May Day processions since 1954. Again, during all the bannered hoopla of this May Day I sought out pictures or references to China's atom bomb, to her international status as a nuclear power. There was nothing. The small black and white picture in Canton was to be the only time I saw a picture of the atom bomb displayed, and with that picture there was no caption. I left China May 14, the same day that China's second atom bomb was exploded. However, friends from the tour who remained in Canton a couple of extra days said there were open announcements in the newspapers and in banners

78

proclaiming the scientific accomplishment with enormous pride.

After a series of juggling and acrobatic acts, at which the Chinese are highly skilled, we went to a large, open-air Greek-style theater for another brief session of Peking modern opera. This time it was the Japanese who were getting a going-over.

Like so much Chinese theater today, the opera was based on an incident during the Japanese occupation. There was no admission fee and thousands of people of all ages crowded the vast amphitheater. Later, I was to see half a dozen plays and operas in which the Chinese landlords, "imperialistic capitalists," and the Kuomintang troops of Chiang Kai-shek were targets for identical abuse.

Confusion and irony had been added to the Canton incident of the portrayal of the sniveling GI, in the form of constant reassurances from everyone we met that China is "truly a friend of the American people but not of the American government."

It is a fact that I never saw or heard the word "American" or "U.S." without the word "imperialism" following it. The Chinese appeared to be making a consistent effort to maintain a distinction between the government and the people. Always it was the "aggressive American government" or the "American imperialists." The sole exception to this was the sniveling GI in the Canton play. The characterization of the GI was, however, little different from that of the Japanese troops depicted in the occupation themes: it was apparent that they felt the wearing of a government uniform removed any personal identity whatsoever from the bearer and invested in him only those qualities that characterized the *government* as seen through the eyes of the Chinese.

I asked several times how it was possible to draw a distinction between a government and the masses who freely and consistently return that same government to power?

To this I received no satisfactory answer.

Now, sitting in the park with the group and Yu and Li beside me, I was asked how I had liked the anti-Japanese occupation play. Obviously, they were remembering my reaction to the Canton play.

"I was glad to see it, in a way, after that offensive and totally unfair play in Canton. The way things are shaping up you seem to be hopping mad with half the world."

"Mrs. Hobbs," said Yu, "you must remember the Chinese do not have one soldier abroad nor do we have one air base. You would know better than we do perhaps how many American bases there are ringed around the world."

I could hear his words but was distracted by the strangeness of the situation—the park in the heart of Peking, crimson lanterns floating above us, red tails curling in the wind, strange and delicate pipings all around as a score of players blew and plucked. And, sitting beside me, an "old" revolutionary speaking what I believe to this day to be commonly held thoughts in China.

"We wonder at times how the American people would feel if our fleet was off the coast of Maine all year. Or who would the Americans call 'aggressive' if our planes were to sweep over New York or San Francisco as American planes go over our territory at Hainan Island; or if we had troops and arms at the Mexican border."

To this I replied:

"The Americans would not like it. But international law has always been based on force and not on morality. The Americans have a deeper social conscience, and more means of implementing it, than any power the world has previously seen. Who knows how China will act if it ever becomes the most powerful nation in the world? America is not interested in your territory. Had she wanted territory she could have seized Japan and large areas of Europe for herself after the last

80

war. Instead, America gave the devastated countries aid to help build themselves back up. Look at the standard of living in Japan today: has any conqueror ever treated its vanquished enemy more benevolently?"

The ritualistic reaction to this could be summed up:

"We will never be aggressive when we gain greater power. Nor will we carry on any expansion: that is determined by our socialist system. As for Japan, its wealth is based on the American dollar."

"You are concerned with the masses," I said, "and for the masses do you really think it matters when the end result is that they are better off than they have ever been before? Surely this is the criterion by which your system makes a judgment?"

Once such a remark to another official—Yu would never have been so blunt—ended with my being told:

"Mrs. Hobbs, you are either naïve or prejudiced."

But this was May Day, a day of festivity.

"Come," said Yu with a great and toothy grin, "there is yet much to see!"

That was Yu's understatement of the year, for after leaving the park we went to see the Summer Palace, the great sprawling estate built in 1894 by the luxury-loving concubine who became the Dowager Empress Tzu Hsi. Rumored to have cost $50,000,000, the money was intended to build a navy for China but the capricious lady blew it on a whim instead. China is still short of the navy, but as I told Yu by way of comfort, most Western powers have gone through several navies since that date and none of them can boast of a Summer Palace!

Here thousands of youthful parents, neatly dressed and groomed, picnicked with their beribboned youngsters around the lake, four miles in circumference. Others paddled lazily along in boats decorated with flags and lanterns. It was a rare sight indeed. There was nothing modern or mechanized to be seen. The palace, a series of pavilions, halls and towers, sprawling at different levels up the side of a hill, could have been sitting there for centuries, as could the people moving leisurely on the lake with their red lanterns. I wondered if it were possible in any other leading capital of the world to find such a large recreational area where the simple pleasures were so totally divorced from any dependence on modern times.

The Summer Palace was the empress' idea of an earthly paradise.

We entered the palace grounds through a crimson-painted wooden portico. There must have been forty large buses in the parking lot and more cars than I had seen accumulated anywhere in China. Mingling with hundreds of holiday-makers, we wound our way through ancient bronze lions, passed marble balustrades and into the internationally re-nowned Painted Gallery. This long, curving archway, with its graceful wooden columns and carved knee-high side-railing, is carved and painted on every inch of its curved roofway. Hun-dreds of brightly painted scenes, crammed with the most minute detail, have been brought back to life in recent years through skillful restoration. On one side is the lake, on the other leafy trees from all over the world.

Here, too, more than in the downtown parks, were hun-dreds of older citizens. The palace is some miles out of town near the western hills and I wondered if the buses were for these elderly people, for when we returned to the city, we passed hundreds of younger people walking the miles-long journey back.

The men, some with calf-length tunics over their slacks, invariably wore black: their wispy white beards lent an air of antiquity and wisdom. It is a fact that the Chinese have little body hair: the men in our group shaved off a couple of dozen sprouting hairs from the chin or upper lip every four or five days and that was it. The wispy beards of these ancients probably represented a lifelong growth! Perhaps they had been allowed to keep them as a privilege, as I did not see one young person in China with a beard. Moustaches were almost as rare.

Here too were scores of elderly women, also in black, their white hair drawn back in a bun, hobbling along with the mincing steps of those whose feet had been bound when children. It hurt just to look at the mutated stump in its neat white sock and soft black shoe. The binding of feet was outlawed—not always successfully—even before the Communists took over, but thousands of victims are still visible in any city. I noticed that Yu did not like us to pay any special attention to these ladies: it was as if he anticipated some show of insensitivity, perhaps a pointed finger or loud remark, from tourists, or perhaps felt ashamed of this cruel vestige of former days. None of us dared to take a picture.

On the other hand, all of us had noticed that the Chinese women often looked at our feet, somewhat surreptitiously of course. We assumed they were looking at our strange high-heeled shoes—Chinese women wear either soft cloth shoes of black felt and corduroy, or stout leather walking shoes—but as it continued when we wore sandals or gym shoes, we faced the awful fact that they were fascinated by our huge, flat feet!

Now, in a square off the Painted Gallery, we were taken for our "treat"—a play staged by students of the Peking University dealing with President Johnson's Baltimore speech, in which he offered to enter into peace negotiations with North Viet Nam. We were given front seats, and although we had seemingly wandered aimlessly and at our own individual pace from one park to another, our tour must have been most carefully thought out. For we were no sooner seated than the signal was given and the play began.

Wearing an Uncle-Sam morning suit, the caricature of the President was accompanied by offstage gongs and fast-paced patter. President Johnson (with a kerchiefed matron in the background carrying a basket of both doves and bombs) called in "Ambassador Maxwell D. Taylor" and "Secretary of Defense Robert S. McNamara."

A member of the American press, snap-brim hat on the back of his head, a loose tie and a garish shirt, joined the trio, a notebook and poised pencil in hand. Aware of the extraordinary position I was in—what would these kids have felt or said had they known I was a member of the American press?—I nonetheless moved almost to the feet of the actors and, crouching on the stage area, took pictures of the highly theatrical antics which, for sheer subtlety, were reminiscent of the silent flicks.

They pondered, argued, flew from one solution of the Viet Nam situation to another, all with wild gestures, fast patter, offstage gongs. The President held out a carrot with an ingratiating smile; behind his back he had a stick.

His speech was brief and to the (Chinese) point.

"Uncles and Aunties (ladies and gentlemen), you must accept my unconditional peace talks conditionally. We, like you, want peace and as soon as I am President of the whole world we shall have peace."

Later that night we attended the fireworks display in Tien An Men Square sharing, with other international "guests," standing space on the broad steps that flank the crimson and gold Gate of Heavenly Peace. There was some evidence, or at least display, of the "union of nationalities"—equality and integration with minority groups—that China claims. At least representatives from Mongolia and the far west provinces were there in force in cobalt blue dresses, knee-length boots and sometimes extraordinarily intricate headdresses.

One of the features of the fireworks display, which was flamboyant and brilliantly staged, was the discipline of the crowds. There were no barriers in the square, and no police cars or mounted police.

Each large concrete block in the square is numbered:

there was no shoving, no confusion. Those in the front row facing the gate maintained a straight line without effort, despite the 700,000 persons behind them.

Just as striking was the lack of litter. Probably most of Peking's 7 million inhabitants were on the streets and in the parks some time that day: the total absence of litter was phenomenal. I asked Li Tieh-fei how such cleanliness had been achieved.

"Education," he replied. "Our people were not so clean before."

I can see education eventually maintaining hygienic standards, but I think a few arms must have been twisted to provide the original momentum.

It was now ten o'clock and the night had turned quite chilly. Earlier that day when leaving the hotel, I had asked the group to wait while I went up in "the elevator to get a sweater." An Australian would have said "gone up in the lift to get a jumper."

"Sometimes you speak like a Yank, Lisa," one of the group had remarked.

Now, standing watching the fireworks explode over the city, someone handed around a bag of "lollies."

Forgetful again I took mine and passed them on to Li.

"Have a candy, Li Tieh-fei," I said, and he took it and asked:

"And what, Lisa Hobbs, is the difference between a lolly and a candy?"

"Candy," I said, "is an Americanism."

"I am aware of such difference in speech," he said. "I was taught English at Peking University by a Canadian."

A little while later he looked at me sideways and remarked:

"You don't look Australian."

"You don't look Chinese," I said and went to bed with a headache.

8

The Sunday was overcast:
the silent city seemed to have aged centuries overnight.

I thought perhaps the grayness was only in me, for during the night I had awakened with a clear and frightening thought: suppose the Chinese authorities were aware of my identity and just weren't letting on? That they had run a cross check—the Foreign Ministry was only yards away from our hotel—and were having a little fun at my expense? Ridiculous, I told myself, and pulled the blankets over my head.

Down at breakfast I looked for Yu Shang-ven and Li Tieh-fei in the faint hope that routine morning greetings would give the lie to my pregnant, yet still embryonic, anxiety. But they were nowhere to be seen: it was their day off, we were told, and they were home with their wives and children. Or down at the office, I thought, going feverishly through the files!

Our schedule, with Mrs. Chia and a tall, slim, bespectacled young man called Chin, as translators, called for a daylong tour of various points of interest in the city. I wanted to go to a service at Peking's Christian Church and join the group later at the Museum of Chinese History, but such a deviation seemed to cause so much extra work that I decided to go with the group instead.

The museum is one of the ten buildings built in ten months for the tenth anniversary of the new regime in 1959. It is divided into two sections, modern and ancient. With Chin and Lois Carter, wife of a Melbourne attorney, I went to the modern section where the relics of the Long March are housed. Even this slight deviation from the schedule meant special permission and a delay. There is an entrance fee of a few cents into the museum, but Mrs. Chia had already gone in with the rest of the group on the tour ticket. We were left standing outside while Chin went back and forth and special calls were made.

Mao Tse-tung has said that "bureaucracy is dung," but time and time again I noticed there was no slack allowed for any deviation from routine. If bureaucracy is truly dung, there's an awful lot of cleaning up yet to be done in Peking.

The Long March is a thundering historical epic by any standard. It started October 16, 1934, a vast strategic retreat of 90,000 men from the encircling forces of Chiang Kai-shek in southwest China. It ended 6,000 miles to the north in Shensi Province, one year and nine days later. Only 7,000 men survived country as cruel and capricious as any in the world— for the route covered territory in which all the violent grossness of nature was encompassed—jungles and swamps, ice-capped mountain ranges, boiling rivers and deserts that hadn't seen rain in years, and everywhere sickness and starvation.

The relics of the march are of a peculiar nature. They are tattered, fragile, shredded—twisted pieces of iron, jackets that are bundles of rags, ropes eaten through with stress, all conveying a damp, matted quality like goods delivered up from the tomb. Thirty years have elapsed since the Long March ended, but the difference in China, politically, socially and economically, could well be the difference of centuries, and the relics manage to convey this feeling vividly.

The museum was crowded, as was every museum and art gallery I visited. Groups moved from section to section, while the guides, specially trained young girls in pigtails and navy slacks and jackets, used long pointers to illustrate their lectures. The groups didn't seem to represent one segment exclusively: there were students, or couples on an outing; workers who were obviously worse off than the students; many older men, but not too many older women. They moved from spot to spot in silence and watched and listened with a fearful intensity. Sometimes, turning to move, they would brush against me and step back a pace in sheer surprise. This was in such contrast to the rather sophisticated indifference we usually met with on the street that I now chalked a lot of the indifference down to a mixture of emotions rather than none at all, or—judging by their purposeful pace—they were just too busy to stop and stare.

From the museum we crossed Tien An Men Square— nearly 100 acres in area—into the Great Hall of the People, another ten-month project.

Wandering through this vast, cavernous structure, I thought that here indeed is a quality that the Americans and Chinese share in common—a pride in building the biggest project in the shortest time. Mrs. Chia did a masterful job in reeling off the statistics—the frontage is 1,100 feet long; the banquet hall seats 5,000; the twenty-two reception rooms, each representing a province and decorated in products from that province, large enough to hold 500 persons; the Great Hall itself, which seats 10,000 persons. It was like a tour of New York City for members of a building convention.

Fourteen thousand workers were employed in its construction, and thousands of volunteers gave up their evenings and weekends to lend a hand, said Mrs. Chia.

In any case, the convention hall itself, where the 3,000 members of the National People's Congress meet once a year, impresses by its sheer vastness. There are 5,000 seats on the ground floor, and above it, two curved and unsupported balconies which seat, respectively, 3,000 and 2,000 spectators. It is here that China's modern theatrical epic, *The East Is Red, the Sun Is Rising,* is staged with its cast of 3,000.

All seats on the ground floor are equipped with earphones for simultaneous translation of up to ten languages, including English and Russian, the two most popular foreign languages.

We sat down to try out the seats for comfort when a funny and inexplicable incident occurred. A Coca-Cola ad flashed on the screen before us! Had President Johnson stepped out from the wings we could scarcely have been more surprised. Coca-Cola in the Great Hall of the People!

"Counterrevolutionaries at work?" I asked Mrs. Chia.

She laughed. Chia was one of the few women I met in China who held an official job and could still laugh.

"They are getting ready to make a film of 'The East Is Red,'" she said. "They must be getting ready ... perhaps it is a slide to get everything in focus ... really, I don't know what it is."

We never did find out: it became an inscrutable, Oriental mystery!

The tourist-interpreter relationship is a strange one. Sometimes, for days at a time, one is left totally dependent on the companionship of a complete stranger. In our case, we had the same two interpreters with us throughout the tour; but sometimes, as in Peking, they had other work to do, or a day off, and total strangers would step in to fill out the days. How fruitful and pleasant the day was often depended on pot luck —the personality and competence of the interpreter. As they are all cadres—men and women who receive exact and special training in the upholding and promulgation of the Marxist-

Leninist doctrine—their political status is considered completely reliable. It also means, however, that conversations readily assume a stilted, unreal dialogue form that quite frequently develops into a sort of verbal one-upmanship. The covert nature of this contest could become quite a strain: added to it was the unsettling knowledge that the gist of the conversations was being recorded on the interpreter's cortex to be played back later that night!

With Mrs. Chia, one always had the feeling that you knew how the conversation would go each night in her report to party officials. Her reactions were instant and direct. She would go beyond the usual good-natured bantering under which we disguised what we really thought, to enter into conversations that were almost like serious debates—a rare thing with a Chinese interpreter. Usually, you got so far and then the curtain dropped: spontaneous human reaction was something we came to treasure.

After we returned to the hotel for lunch I begged off the afternoon tour. I was beginning to suffer from what, south of the border, is called Montezuma's revenge. Food shot through me like an arrow.

There are no food or water restrictions in China. We were assured there was nothing to fear from either fresh or uncooked vegetables, that one could eat them as freely as one did anywhere in Europe or the United States. Considering that our neighbors in Mexico still can't risk eating their vegetables uncooked, this is a remarkable achievement in scientific standards. Furthermore, the tap water in all the tourist cities is safe, which certainly can't be said for some areas of Europe, all of Mexico and almost all of Asia.

I had, however, failed to take the most elementary precaution of a daily dose of a bacteria-reducing drug, a wise step when there is any change in diet or in water, even when the food and water are pure. Some other members on the tour had,

90

some hadn't, but I was the only one in the group weakened enough to take to bed.

I told Chia all I wanted was some medicine, I didn't want a doctor. But it wasn't possible to get medicine without a doctor; besides, there were two doctors who lived in the Nationalities Hotel to attend exclusively to staff and guest needs.

Later that afternoon I awoke to an extraordinary sight. Two women doctors, their faces in white masks, their heads in white caps, their forms draped in white down to the floor, were peering over me intently.

"Hold it," I said, and rolled off the bed and took their picture. Chin, the other interpreter, was with them; he said they didn't mind the picture as long as their masks were up!

For the first part of the examination, Chin remembered the restrictions that Westerners ceremoniously observe during a medical examination. Asking the most detailed and embarrassing questions, he stared politely out the window. But, as time passed, he drifted back into the center of the room and ended up standing by the bed pleasantly chattering. My exposed condition meant absolutely nothing. Finally, the doctors spoke to Chin and came up with a diagnosis of "a little indigestion."

It was a classic case of literal translation. Clutching a sheet, I tried to explain that it was true the food was not being digested, but we didn't call that "indigestion." Trying to get indigestion, I clutched my chest and burped gently. The three stood in solemn silence watching me.

Finally Chin said:

"What is the matter now, Mrs. Hobbs?"

A little while later, four separate packages of drugs arrived —two different kinds of tablets, one packet of pills, and an envelope of capsules. It looked like a kill-or-cure campaign but by morning I was completely well again.

We were to visit a commune that day. On our way, at my

request, we stopped at the Military Museum of the Chinese People's Revolution. I wanted to see for myself the three American robot spy planes which had either crashed or been brought down over Chinese territory.

They were assembled in a central courtyard and all around the roped-off area the youth of China passed in thousands. Trucks of soldiers arrived while we were there and when we left they were still lined up waiting to see the "proof" of America's "aggressive intent."

I found this a profoundly upsetting experience: in fact, when I moved in close, ducking under the roped-off area, to get a closeup of the manufacturer's nameplate engraved on a steel plaque (Ryan of San Diego), I found that my hand was shaking. The Chinese had set up white cardboard plaques with black arrows pointing to the cameras nestling in the front of the plane. Lying now, glittering sightlessly in the weak sun, they looked alien and ugly. Despite my continuing irritation at the anti-American propaganda, I left the museum thinking over what Yu had said the previous day, and wondering how it would feel if several Russian- or Chinese-built planes crashed in the Midwest.

I was interested to see, as I crossed the courtyard, a couple of old American B-25 bombers. Curious to find out if they were some of Billy Mitchell's old planes captured by the Japanese and left in Peking in their retreat, I asked around, but neither our interpreters nor the man at the door seemed to know.

Back in the bus—a couple of the Australians had refused to come in because they said it was all "propaganda"—a lively discussion on the use of spy planes followed.

Ironically enough, Mrs. Chia expressed my thoughts when she said with no little disgust:

"How would the rest of the world like it if we sent spy planes up over their countries?"

Paul Morawetz, the Australian economist, said it was foolish to adopt a moral attitude about it, that the spy planes were simply an improvement on the old trench-coat method of spying.

"All countries have spies," he said.

"We don't have one spy plane up," said Mrs. Chia.

"Because you don't own one," said Morawetz.

"Oh!" said Mrs. Chia, her breath expulsed in a flash of anger. I felt that if she had been French she would have hit Morawetz on the head with her umbrella. Instead, she just stomped it on the floor.

The rest of our ride to the Vietnamese Friendship Commune went peacefully enough. It was only 12 miles from the heart of the city, yet the area was so rural and isolated it could have been 100 miles away.

We were met by director Kua, a tough little weather-beaten man, who spoke clearly and intensely. His commune seemed to be a real "going" affair with 4,000 cattle, half of which were the local Peking black and white cow with a daily output of about 14 U.S. quarts of milk.

In contrast to the East Flower Commune outside Canton, all agricultural work on this commune was mechanized. Kua said there were forty-two tractors (those I saw up for repair were Rumanian) and that, as a result, the grain output had increased 60 per cent in the past eight years.

The commune, which comprised 7,000 families, or 30,000 persons, in what was formerly thirty-five separate villages, also boasted a variety of industrial enterprises. There were six factories producing farm tools, a brick factory, a factory producing chemical fertilizer (using, I understood Kua to say, a combination of potash, sulphur and calcium).

"We also have a pickle mill and make bean noodles, a very popular food with the Chinese," said Kua. "We also have our own flour mill."

Kua said the big problem of the commune's early years was water.

"The Ashe River runs from east to west across the north edge of the commune," he said. "In 1960, we had a big flood, but this was followed by three years of drought. However, before the flood, relying on our own efforts, we had built a dike across the river.

"Nine years out of ten the people here had sorrows before the commune was formed," said Kua. "Such floods and droughts as those in the early sixties would have cost many of them their lives. But with the dike, ten pumping stations that we had built, fifty wells that we had sunk, we all survived—and well."

This commune also seemed further advanced in the social amenities than the East Flower Commune. A team regularly visited the different villages to show films; there were seventeen television sets (Peking has one channel) and we were told that 50 per cent of the residents owned bicycles, while the rest owned radios. I noticed some of the bicycles parked around the commune workshop area were the least expensive 175 yuan ($87) variety. Many of them were rickety and rusted. The only radio that I saw on the commune—at the Home of Respect for the Aged—was the cheapest kind, the small, 50 yuan ($25) model.

Formerly, none of the residents had had electric light: now all but 5 per cent had electricity. Every village maintained its own primary school, while two middle schools (high schools) had been built to serve the entire commune. There were four Homes of Respect for the Aged for those without children or relatives.

Each person in the commune received 450 pounds of grain a year plus an average annual income of 300 yuan ($150). This income did not include other income that might come from the sale or exchange of goods such as chickens and vegetables raised on their small private plots, which comprised 5 per cent of the commune's total acreage.

Walking across the commune recreation area, I asked Kua about a woman who had passed and greeted him.

"There were seven people in her family before Liberation," he said. "All hands bent to the farm, but still there was not enough to eat, never any clothes and thin, cold bedding. All they owned was a little basin made of iron.

"Now the same family has eight members, four of them manpower, and they have a house and some land, a total income of 1,200 yuan and receive 4,500 pounds of grain. Now they have a wireless set and one bicycle and own an enamel basin."

From the familiarity with which Kua spoke, and the surprising vehemence that entered his voice when he mentioned that "all they owned was a little basin made of iron," I think the woman who had greeted him could have been a member of his own household.

Kua concluded:

"It is because of this sort of thing that the people here always say that without the Communist party and Chairman Mao they could not have had such a happy life."

I do not think that this was just Kua's off-the-cuff contribution to propaganda. This was an extremely well run and prosperous-looking commune. It was interesting to note that the cattle were being kept in the most modern of methods: continuously stalled in huge, one-level red-brick buildings, they were allowed out to wander around a fenced-in yard only for two hour-long periods a day. There they exercised and fed on silage before being returned to their stalls.

There was a fierce-looking bull chained by a loop to a long overhead wire in a nearby yard. The loop allowed him to exercise but within a very restricted area. Semen was taken twice a day and all the cows were artificially inseminated in a nearby laboratory. Cows near full term were put into a special yard where they were carefully watched. After birth, the calves were immediately removed and placed in hay-lined stalls. The mother was put back into the special yard for a few days before being returned to her regular stall. In the interim, junior had graduated from his hay-lined stall into the regular, neck-locking stalls with all the other calves.

On our way to visit a couple of the homes in an adjoining village, we passed a long line of primary-school-age children with tools tossed over their shoulders, marching to the fields.

I asked Kua what he hoped for the future. Did he, for instance, foresee a time when each family would have a separate bathroom instead of a communal shower-room?

The gist of his answer was that this sort of thing, and many others, were part of his vision for the future.

"But what of double bathrooms, like some American families?" I persisted, for I wanted to find out if there was a ceiling to his expectations, or where those expectations lay. But his reply, or the translation to his reply, was lost in the hoots of derision of a couple of the Australian tourists. Knowing the building pace Down Under, the Chinese will have them before the Australians.

We stopped near a couple of homes in a miserably poor village where there had been no building done, it seemed, for centuries. The homes, single or adjoining rooms, were neat and clean, the concrete floors worn smooth. A central stove with ceiling pipes heated the room and one of the pipes ran around the wall and into the *kang*. The top of this *kang* was covered with colorful handmade quilts. In one home we were greeted by a tiny, black-haired lady who looked about fifty; in another, a grandmother, smiling gummily and hauling with her a fat two-year-old boy, showed us her room with pride. She was the boy's grandmother, she said; his mother was working in the fields.

We then went to the Home of Respect for the Aged. Here little, toothless old ladies with bandy legs greeted us with chortles of joy and unmistakable warmth. One took my hand and refused to let go. I wondered what her life had been —born in the time of emperors, dying in a Communist regime. War without ceasing: it seemed a true triumph over nature that she was still here to laugh.

And laugh they did! One was blind; I took her hand and ran it over my face so that she, too, could better join in the occasion. With consummate pride they took us into their rooms (six lived in each), that couldn't have been more humble or cleaner. There was a window, six planks as bed with bedding rolled up at the foot, a stove on which the cooking was done, and a mirror!

The mirror was over the only table in the room; on this all their possessions were neatly stacked into six piles. They each contained such things as a comb, plastic flowers, pictures of scenic views cut from magazines, a scarf. The various tasks of running the room were allotted by mutual vote! The youngest was seventy-three: their hands were rough with labor. Next door were the men and they, too, shook hands and greeted us with a sense of dignity and pride. When I asked Kua why they were in a home and not with their children, he said all had outlived their children and other relatives and had nowhere else to live.

Only two months earlier in California I had done a survey of nursing homes for the San Francisco *Examiner*. The physical conditions of the worst nursing homes I had visited were palatial compared to this: but I did not go into any home within reach of the average aged person's budget where a spirit of integrity and contentment ruled as it did here; of course, I wasn't free in China to visit homes everywhere as I was in the United States. Bereft of everything material that we consider necessary to happiness, they were still able to consider themselves valid contributors to the human scene to the end. China has adopted many Western techniques for living and has been severely criticized for breaking up the family, but all that I saw relative to the aged indicated that China has not abandoned its traditional belief that the aged merit respect.

Driving along the paved highway—straight like all the others and lined with trees painted white to the waist—I found Li Tieh-fei beside me.

"Mrs. Hobbs," he said, and my heart sank because I could tell from the tone of his voice that something serious was coming. "You take many notes; what do you plan to do with them?"

I said that I wrote for small magazines abroad.

"Which ones?" he persisted.

"I really don't think you'd know them."

This was followed by what is commonly known as a "pregnant" silence.

Still he said nothing; I looked out the bus window but in the growing dark all I could see was Li's thoughtful face reflected in the glass.

We were almost outside the hotel when he said:

"You have told us that you lived in America. By your children's ages they must have been born there. Are they American citizens?"

"They have dual citizenship," I said, surprising even myself. I was slipping into a pit of lies and didn't like it one bit.

"Li," I said, "would you please tell Mr. Yu that I would like to talk to him after dinner."

I had decided to send up a trial balloon, to give a little of the truth to see what the traffic would bear.

They both came to my room; it was very formal. We shook hands and then I made tea from the vast thermos. I was in my slippers and shuffled around in silence while they sat, quite at ease and comfortable, and smoked. I felt that I was at one of their criticism-confession meetings. I sat on the side of my bed, took a deep breath and plunged ahead:

"Mr. Yu," I said, "when I applied for a visa I stated I was a free-lance writer. That wasn't strictly honest. Before coming here, an English newspaper asked me if I would do a series of articles on China. I did not say so in my application for fear it would be rejected."

Li translated. There was a moment's silence.

"No objection," came Yu's reply through Li. "We ask only that you be fair and objective and report the good with the bad."

This reaction was better than I could have hoped for. I shook hands with Yu and he departed, followed by Li. Li shook hands as he went through the door, with a pressure, as if of gratitude, and a warmth that had not been there before.

9

There is one characteristic
that makes a visit to Peking memorable, if not astonishing, and that is the surprise one feels in seeing the number of representatives of nations all over the world who freely come and go. Living in America, the tendency is to think of China as isolated; the fact is that we are the ones who are isolated from what is going on in China.

Stand on the steps of the Nationalities—or any other of the city's half-dozen modern hotels—and within an hour a sizable representation of the world can be seen going through the revolving doors.

I'd been prepared for this in a small way. When boarding the Qantas plane in Sydney I asked the elderly man next to me if he was vacationing in Hong Kong.

"No, I'm off to China for my holidays this year," he said. "I've never been there and my friends tell me it's worth the visit."

I asked if he had had any difficulty getting a visa.

"Difficulty?" he said with a trace of disbelief in his voice, as if he hadn't heard correctly. "Not that I know, my travel agency fixed it up."

During my brief visit to Peking—riding up and down in the elevators, chatting in the dining room, running into bargain seekers in the antique specialty shops on the famous Liu Li Chang street—I met tourists and salesmen from Argentina, Australia, Bolivia, Chile, Canada, England, East Germany, France, Holland, Italy, Japan, and a score of African nations.

I also met teachers from several of these countries. They had been imported to teach languages. They were paid 2,000 pounds sterling a year (approximately $6,000), were given eight to ten students and kept these students for four years (at the end of which they were to speak the language fluently).

As far as the tourist trade is concerned, it is still in its infancy. Last year, 2,000 tourists visited China, in contrast to the twenty-six million tourists claimed by Italy. This 2,000 does not include an unknown, but certainly far greater, number of businessmen, bankers, buyers, salesmen, students, teachers, and sundry political fellow travelers.

Although to many people in the United States China appears to have all but dropped from the face of the earth, except as a fear-filled shadow, it is in fact within easy reach of most countries of the world. The Pakistani International Airlines operates direct services twice weekly to Shanghai and Canton from Karachi and Dacca. This PIA route also connects with London, Frankfurt, Geneva, Rome, and Beirut. There are direct air and rail services bringing in passengers from Europe to Peking through Moscow and Ulan Bator. As well, trains run three times a day with passengers between Hong Kong and the border: in September, 1965, China opened negotiations with the British for a direct daily air service between Hong Kong–Canton–Shanghai to help handle the ever-increasing business traffic.

I met one English couple vacationing in Peking with their

two children. They had taken the week-long overland train from Moscow. Chinese trains do not have first, second, and third class anymore. They have de luxe, soft seats and hard seats! This couple had traveled de luxe at the cost of $140 round trip for each adult, half-price for children. The journey, they said, was "quite fabulous, really."

What was the nicest part of the trip?

"Quite frankly," the Britisher said, "it was the total lack of American tourists."

One afternoon, Mrs. Chia told us that there was a distinguished Chinese economist addressing a visiting Japanese trade delegation and we would be welcome to attend the lecture.

It was held in a most comfortably, almost luxuriously, furnished reception room on the top floor. Picture windows, which ran the entire length of the room, opened on to a balcony which, in turn, provided a magnificent view of the city.

The men who are developing China's new economy certainly seem committed to a go-it-alone philosophy—a fierce independence that turns its back on help from any country. But the extent of this independence didn't come home to me until I met Dr. Yung Lung kuei. Yung, an economist at Peking University, is vice-president of the China Council for the Promotion of International Trade.

Second only to the amount of speculation about loss of freedom in Communist countries is the speculation about economic conditions. Because Yung is a high official in China, I would like to repeat what he said, in the way he said it, to try to give the reader the freedom to believe or disbelieve this economist's summation of some aspects of his country's condition. I took the quotations down, word for word, in shorthand.

Yung said that China had not had "a fair chance" to

102

demonstrate what has been done, or what can be done, because of natural and political calamities.

Describing the years 1958–60 as showing "the greatest development in production," Yung said:

"But while we were advancing forward we also met with difficulty. We had three natural calamities in 1960. Also the Soviet Government decided to withdraw all its experts in July, 1960. The Soviet stopped our supplies of machines and raw materials, thus causing serious damage to our economy. This caused a temporary but big calamity."

But it also precipitated a far deeper issue, said Yung.

"For the first time we faced the real issue of whether to rely on ourselves or on others. We determined to rely on our own strength to settle all the difficulties. In 1961, we carried out a complete policy of readjustment, consolidation and raising standards. First place was given to increasing both production and quality and by 1964 we had shown all around improvement."

As others did not want to sell machines to China, said Yung, "we decided to make them all ourselves."

He said that China is now self-sufficient in gasoline.

"Now a new upsurge in industry and agriculture is developing. This year, industrial production will increase by 11 per cent, agriculture by 5 per cent, perhaps more. It is now only May Day. Right now we are working on a draft of the third Five-Year Plan which we begin next year."

Yung then touched on what he called "a problem of production."

"In the development of production the first question is how to handle the relationship between men and machines. Some people say 'technique should be all important and man secondary.' We hold that men are more important than machines, that all machines are merely creations of man. If the people of the whole country bring into full play their ability to think, speak and act, and do away with superstitions many new methods will come. Revolutionary zeal should be combined with scientific spirit.

"The wisdom of the collective is better than that of individuals, that is why we advocate leadership, technology, and the masses. We must learn to emulate the best and help those who fall behind. So, in the past few years, we have many new inventions, such as the microscope with an enlargement of 200,000 times. The new products we have made have received very little publicity." (At this point I bit the end of my ballpoint pen to stop from grinning, for I thought of the publicity his statements were unwittingly about to receive.)

"Next year, if there are no obstacles (here a brief reference to Chiang Kai-shek was lost in the babble of translations), we will exhibit in Japan. If we are not complacent we can develop very quickly. We emphasize self-reliance: we must rely solely on the efforts of our own people. This does not mean we have a closed-door policy. We now have trade relations with 120 countries and areas. We do not want to trade with the United States, either with its government or with individual capitalists.

"We paid back our debts to the USSR of 1,400 million rubles last January 30. The end of the year has not yet come but, according to our estimates, the USSR now owes China. So we are not only getting better and better but also paying off our debts as well.

"What policies do we develop in art and culture? A socialist one. To be frank, we do not welcome the American way of life. We do not negate all the heritage of culture left over by the old China. In art we have new creations, such as Peking opera with a contemporary theme. Art and literature are not a recreational means but are a means of educating the whole people, especially the young.

"Fifteen years is a short time. Our country is still young. Old things still exist but they are dwindling every day. We lack experience and welcome your criticisms and suggestions."

As Yung spoke, the official translation was given in Japanese. Our translators labored in a veritable babel. Questions were called for. I asked if there were any conditions under which China would trade with the United States, if the United States wanted to trade.

"It is hard to say," replied Yung quite affably. "First the United States should really withdraw from Taiwan. At that time we should consider."

In Canton, where I had visited the Chinese Export Commodities Hall for the spring exhibition and later, in Shanghai, at the Industrial Exhibition, I saw concrete proof both of China's emphasis on self-reliance and her need to upgrade quality, if not in heavy industry at least in the department-store type of consumer merchandise.

There were 3,000 items at the Canton fair, ranging from pottery and carpets to motor scooters and human hair. Quality went the full range from poor to outstanding, with the majority of products hitting a fair, but not first quality, mean.

Not so the heavy industry products from the steel-producing areas of Shanghai, which I was to see in a couple of days, but which I will mention now in relation to the professor's talk. Even to my nonspecialist eye, quality appeared to be higher. Buyers with whom I later spoke said that China is now producing some of the cheapest and best precision instruments in the world.

This display in the unfortunately named Sino-Soviet Friendship Building—"we don't intend to change the name," an interpreter said quite brusquely when asked—included shipbuilding (by models), hypodermic needles, heart-lung machines (a machine used to keep the body alive during open-heart surgery), motorized pedicabs, dye-casting ma-

105

chines, lathes, the microscope the professor referred to, static accelerators, hydraulic presses, a Phoenix automobile (a one-piece construction job with white-wall tires), ball bearings and so on.

The motorized pedicabs are being introduced at the rate of 4,000 a year, our guide told us. Anything quicker would create havoc in the pedicab industry. As for the Phoenix, it was not really in production. "Just a few official cars," he said. I gathered that, like some of the other products, it was more to show what China can do rather than what she is actually doing on any large scale.

Also in Shanghai I was to see the 12,000-ton hydraulic press which so epitomizes everything central to the revolution.

The Chinese regard this massive, 75-foot high steel monster—which is capable of turning out 250 ton dies—as proof of their independence from other nations in industrial progress. It is located at a place with the fascinating name of Chong Xing Ji Qu Chang—Shanghai Heavy Machinery Plant.

The story the Chinese tell of this press is that it was built from a blueprint that nobody could understand and all the parts—such as the five-ton screw cap—as well as the required tools, were designed and made as the "engineers, scientists, and steel workers" worked together unraveling the print.

Running jumps in industry and China's desire to trade, however, have done little to ease the path of the overseas buyer who, sitting at the bargaining table in Peking, finds himself wandering blindfolded in the heart of an economy that lacks any means of its own to determine a fair selling price in a competitive international market.

I spoke to buyers in all the cities I was in, particularly in Peking. They all told the same story—that the Chinese were eminently honorable in their dealings. But the buyer must choose the selling price he is about to suggest with agonizing care, for the Chinese are capable of abrupt action, of quitting a conference without warning if the hapless buyer suggests a selling price which falls far short of their expectations.

The buyer is then left with the alternative of getting permission to stay on in Peking and trying to reopen negotiations —usually a heart-breaking and futile task—or of facing the fact that he's a loser this time and going home.

"The trouble is," one Australian buyer told me, "you never know whether your bid is 100 per cent below their expectations or 100 per cent above it. In some of their smaller items, handkerchiefs for instance, they are still 100 per cent below the Spanish market. The shoes are half the price of Australian shoes and twice the quality. Every time I make a visit the quantity, quality, and variety of goods available have increased."

I ran into this same buyer in the passenger lounge of the Manila Airport in the Philippine Islands a couple of weeks after our conversation in Peking. I happened to mention that I was a newspaper reporter, a fact he hadn't known before, and he asked the name of my paper. When I said Hearst, he sat bolt upright and asked if the Chinese had known when they issued me a visa. I said no, whereupon in great agitation he moved to another lounge chair, buried himself in a newspaper and refused to speak to me again. The only explanation I had for his behavior was that he had a good thing going in his business dealings with the Chinese and didn't want to do anything that might in any way jeopardize his good relationship.

I spoke to another buyer, an Englishman, in Peking. He first went to China five years ago to look at optical instruments and has since built up an extensive business. He said the Chinese frankly admitted they had no idea what their products should sell for. He said, however, he never had any worry about buying at a fair price.

"We all sit down around a table. There are formal statements made on both sides. Tea is served. The Chinese then produce catalogues which illustrate similar type Swiss and German instruments. Invariably, they ask me what I consider would be a fair profit. In that way, we eventually reach an agreeable price."

All buyers emphasized the extreme patience that must be exercised through hours of exhaustive translations.

"It would almost drive you crazy," one buyer, scouting shoes, told me in Shanghai. "There is no way of telling from the expression on their faces whether they are delighted or furious with the offer you are making. Nor does their tone of voice reveal the slightest nuance of feeling: nor can you tell what a Chinese is thinking and feeling by his tone of voice as the intonations of the Chinese language are totally different."

The same buyer said his first buying trip, involving days of niggling negotiations, handicapped and slowed down constantly through labored translations, ended up with the Chinese shouting at him.

"I just sat on the edge of my chair and thought: 'Damn it! You've really messed this deal up!' But when it was all over, instead of this official stalking off in a storm, he burst into smiles and shook my hand. We'd made a really good deal—but you'd never have guessed it!"

Typical of the way in which business is conducted is the fact that on April 14, one day before the Canton fair opened, the Chinese Government sent telegrams to every foreign buyer in the world with whom they did business and announced a flat price increase of 20 per cent on all products over last year's price. This also illustrates China's upswinging status and confidence in the world market.

My own acquaintance with the Chinese economy was brief indeed. It occurred in a silk factory in the garden city of Soochow. After we had been escorted through the factory, we were taken to a room where bolts of fine and colorful pure silk, as well as the traditional richly embroidered brocade, were on display.

We asked what a meter (a little over one yard) of this silk would cost.

The factory manager looked puzzled; the interpreter repeated the question.

"I do not know," said the factory manager.

We smiled, assuming he hadn't understood the question, and asked Li Tieh-fei to repeat it.

"He doesn't know," said Li, as if we weren't understanding.

"Ask him if his wife went into a store how much would she have to pay to buy one meter of this cloth," I said.

Again the factory manager said he frankly didn't know.

None of us could accept the answer he was giving us: it didn't make sense. But it was possible that his wife, if he had one, didn't buy silk, or that it was unobtainable, or that he really didn't know what price the stores put on it for retail sale.

"Then tell us," we asked, "what is the wholesale price of a meter of this silk?"

"I do not know," the factory manager said quite affably but showing signs of wanting to walk on and cut off our inquiries. Apparently our questions made no more sense to him than his answers made to us. "We do not have any such thing as a wholesale price. The silk is delivered here, we make it up. It leaves the factory. The next lot comes in; we make that up. When it leaves here, I do not necessarily know where it goes. It goes where the government says. I know nothing about price."

In certain ways, the Chinese economy isn't good or bad. It isn't an economy at all by Western standards. There seemed to be no doubt, however, that it is succeeding year by year in its fundamental task of raising both the quantity and quality of production.

10

I rose early the next day,
dressed in slacks and jacket, and slipped out of the hotel hours before breakfast.

Peking is at its best in that brief period between the passing of the dawn and the arrival of the day. The air, totally free of the sound of traffic or the gaseous smells of automobiles, is gray and damp. Unlike almost any other great city in the world, Peking wakes softly. Years ago pigeons, with homemade flutes attached to their tails, would swoop through the air, and light and joyous music would fall to the earth with the first rays of the sun. Sadly, the pigeons, with all other grain-eating birds and rodents, have been eliminated. Yet, if the first rays of the sun now warm the earth in silence, at least they do not light on bodies lying in the street, half-dead from starvation.

When the cold gray mist lifts, the trees, five and six deep on both sides of the main boulevards, frame an extraordinary sight. Hundreds of residents, old and young, workers and students, are seen in various positions of *tai chi chwan*, the traditional, philosophically oriented Chinese calisthenics. It looks like an ancient frieze that the dawn has raised to a slow

110

and languid life. There the people stand, making the strange and subtle movements among the limpid shadows of the trees, like underwater plants moved by a slow tide. Sometimes a man breaks off and walks briskly off to business; a student glances at his watch and dashes off for the bus; the elderly continue the timeless gestures. Some minded that I stood to watch and withdrew to another area; others were lost in thought.

What was this the old man in black was doing, his wispy white beard unmoved by one slowly raising leg: was it Golden Cock Stands on One Leg? And here the black-braided college student, who breaks a rule of the game by smiling at me with white and perfect teeth, as her body moves back in a circular swivel: is this Step Back and Repulse Monkey? Or the brown-skinned middle-aged woman in patched slate-gray clothes whose arms move out and head goes down with the grace of a swan: surely—Wild Horse Tosses Mane. A short ruddy-faced man finishes Snake Creeps Down before he looks at me and moves away to another spot: a middle-aged woman in beige slacks and jacket, prosperous looking by comparison, with rimless glasses and pale face, completes Hit the Tiger.

All these apparently languid movements bear appropriate names, based as they are on the imitation of movements by tigers, birds, monkeys, bears, and other animals. They are nothing new, dating back to the fifth century B.C., although they were not systematized until the Sung Dynasty (960–1127). Derived from a Taoist philosophy of nonviolent resistance, the principle of stress underlies all gestures—the unity of the *yin* (negative) and the *yang* (positive), or the fusing into harmony of opposite elements. The mind must be clear of everything except the movements, which must be rhythmic and circular, the body must rotate from the hip joint and all breathing must be through the nose. Small wonder the Chinese call it the Grand Ultimate Exercise.

It is interesting to note that the theory of stress, more specifically of contradictions, is decisive in Chinese Communist thinking. One of the most closely studied essays by Mao Tse-tung is *On Contradictions*. There are two types, he said, antagonistic, which is resolvable only by force, and nonantagonistic, which can be changed by "discussion, criticism and education." The latter means involves confrontation between opposites, tensions, solutions, and new tensions in a never-ending confrontation that stimulates progress. I could not help but wonder as I watched the *tai chi chuan* movements whether *On Contradictions* was not, in fact, a Marxist reinterpretation of an old Chinese schema.

I was often to notice on these walks, no matter what the time of day, crocodile files of children of all ages out with their kindergarten teachers or supervisors. They were all plump and healthy looking, and their clothes were neat and clean, and in view of what their condition might well have been had they lived before Liberation it might appear petty to balk at their apparent lack of home life. For I had no doubts that many of these children—groups of thirty boys about eight years of age out at ten o'clock on May Day Eve; groups of a dozen straggling toddlers under the care of two youthful-looking girls in the parks on Sunday—lived in state-run schools and nurseries and were being raised away from their parents.

I asked Li Tieh-fei about it and he said casually that he didn't know what groups I had seen but that they most likely were from boarding schools. His own child, he said, attended a nursery. He took him there himself Monday morning and collected him Saturday at noon. He was four years old. It wasn't unusual for a child to have twenty-four-hour-a-day care: the parents could visit any time they wished.

I frankly said I didn't think it was much of an idea and

touched on the dangers of institutionalization. The idea meant nothing to him.

"You should see him," he laughed. "He is so happy. And all his little friends have different personalities. Chinese children are not conformist. You have said yourself how different all the interpreters are."

"But they weren't raised in nurseries, but by their own mothers and fathers who had probably never heard of Marx and Lenin."

And there the conversation ended.

Later, I discussed the matter with a woman interpreter. She had elected to keep her own children at home, yet approved the day-and-night nursery system.

"Mrs. Hobbs, you do not understand our problems. We have barely started, yet already men and women just a few years younger than I do not remember what it was like before Liberation. They do not know the meaning of the landlord. They do not know that an American in a motor car ran over a Chinese and was never brought to court. They do not know that a Chinese girl in Shanghai was raped by an American soldier who went unpunished. How are they to know what it was like before unless we teach them? How are we to accomplish our goals unless they are taught to remember?"

Here, then, was part of the answer: political indoctrination from the beginning was viewed as the only safeguard against the inevitable passage of time and the weakness of revisionism. Certainly, every nursery and classroom I visited was top-heavy with political indoctrination. In one day-care center I saw a group of babies who could barely talk, sitting in a circle while the teacher smilingly asked:

"Where is Chairman Mao?"

Then all together they would point their chubby fingers at Mao's picture on the wall.

113

I believe there are other problems which might have accounted for the acceptance of the nursery-boarding system among the Chinese with whom I spoke—but they were problems of a type that they would not have discussed with me.

I did not see any homes that were larger than one room. Interpreters and specialists of any kind, either male or female, are quite frequently called out of town on government work. The other partner, father or mother, also works; for this person, shift hours might be involved. Living with one or two small children in a room would be hard enough, but under this circumstance, the child might well be better off at a boarding school for five days a week.

These thoughts were among many on my mind as I walked back to the hotel for breakfast that morning.

I wanted very much to see the famous pro-Communist Anna Louise Strong while I was in Peking. Miss Strong is probably the best known of all American residents in China and her *Letter from China* is circulated in the U.S. Back at the hotel I asked Chin, a local interpreter, if he could fix it.

In this instance, and throughout the tour, Luxingshe made every effort to arrange special interviews and appointments wherever practical, even though our group was unofficial and strictly tourist. In certain areas—obviously, the ones they consider more flattering—China is more than willing to share its experiences and experiments with visitors from foreign lands. One of the women was interested in rehabilitation, another in education, while Paul Morawetz asked to talk with a reformed "national capitalist." Special interviews were arranged for each.

Morawetz later said that little was gained from his interview, perhaps because of the necessity of an interpreter, perhaps not. The national capitalist, presumably carefully chosen to meet foreigners, was the former owner of a large heavy-industry plant near Shanghai. He said he was just about bank-

114

rupt in 1947 anyway due to "the Americans flooding the market with all their war surplus tools and machinery in a deliberate attempt to disrupt the economy and seize China's market for herself." His main difficulty wasn't giving up the money but it was giving up his old attitudes and feelings that he was superior to many people. He had eventually "reformed," however, and now lived frugally, but quite contentedly "without any worries," earning top factory salary of 120 yuan ($60) a month as manager of the factory he formerly owned.

As far as my own request was concerned, it was granted without difficulty. At five that afternoon I was in Miss Strong's apartment at the Peace Committee Compound in downtown Peking.

On the table before us, in the comfortable, high-ceilinged room, was a recent copy of *Newsweek* magazine, a novel by Sinclair Lewis, and a book of short stories by Balzac. The furniture was heavy and large. A leather sofa and two deep armchairs were divided by a coffee table. There was a second table, inlaid with mother of pearl. The sideboard was massive and deeply carved: large oriental vases, one about 4 feet high, picked up the vivid cyclamen of a pot of geraniums growing on Miss Strong's desk.

Outside, the dying sun lit up the neglected gardens, once the grounds of the Italian Legation. Only a gatehouse, a keeper, and the twisting gravel drive spoke of the former order of things.

Anna Louise Strong is seventy-nine now. Yet her writing output is greater than it has ever been. Her *Letters* are just part of an outpouring that is translated into Spanish, French, German, Italian, Arabic, and several languages of the new African nations.

Miss Strong entered the room, a formidable dame of the revolution, rather like an old gray battleship. She has followed

115

revolution, and written about it, for over thirty years, so it is hardly surprising that this decade should find her in Peking.

Dressed in a blue shirt-style dress, heavily built, she eyed me appraisingly, almost coldly, as she settled with the slight stiffness of age into an armchair.

I asked her if she planned to go back to America.

She responded swiftly:

"Do you mean do I still regard America as my home? Of course! I am going home the moment the State Department sees fit. I would even go if they made a condition I should not lecture, but I won't go as long as they'll take my passport away from me. If that's the choice I'd rather stay here.

"I was quite aware of the State Department's attitude when I came here several years ago. But I didn't come with the idea of staying more than a couple of years. I left everything in Los Angeles so that I could go back to my home—although it was big and a bit lonely at night—and a place near Desert Hot Springs and a car to run around in."

Did I detect a wistful note? I think so: most people want to go home when the shadows start to fall. Miss Strong is no exception, but stronger than this deep-rooted longing, apparently, is her determination not to let the State Department get her passport while she still might want to use it again.

Her face reflects none of the storms that apparently blow within with unaging passion. She is the daughter of a Methodist minister in Nebraska and if you didn't know it you might guess, for her pale-skinned, round face is mild, her glasses are round and thin-rimmed, and her hair, now white, is drawn back into a neat bun.

Miss Strong spent thirty years in Russia, including a brief stint as a Hearst correspondent during the famines of the early 1920s. During her last visit to Moscow in 1948 she was denounced as an American spy and expelled, only to have the

116

accusation withdrawn by a special Kremlin edict ten years later. If that encounter with Communist sophistry drew blood, there are no scars visible today.

I asked her whether Russia would align with China in any global conflict.

"The differences between Russia and China are very great," she said. "But the Russians could not stand by and see China destroyed. I do not think China could be destroyed: China relies on people. They themselves believe there may be some bombs dropped on them."

Did Miss Strong agree with the Chinese that the U.S. might invade China? No, she did not. Her rejection of this idea, however, was not based on America's traditional disinterest in territorial gain. Rather, she based her argument on the logistical problems such an invasion would encompass.

"It took 580,000 men for the Korean War. To keep 200,000 ready for combat, the American Army must draft at least one million. They would never have the manpower to hold the Chinese mainland. They could do a lot in the destruction of material things—they possess the greatest destructive power the world has ever seen—that, plus a very bad Intelligence service. But after the first bomb was dropped, they would quit, for the world would hate them so."

I was tempted indeed at this stage to say that I lived in the United States and didn't believe for one moment that the people or the government would tolerate such action, despite any Right Wing urgings. Instead, I settled for saying that if the United States did anything as extreme as to bomb China, it would be because the values she held, the goals toward which she was working, necessitated such action. Because of this it was most unlikely that, once embarked on such a course, world opinion could swerve her.

A lifetime of revolution doesn't make for give-and-take

conversation, however, and we were soon in the dusty land of rational polemics. Seeking more fruitful ground, I asked Miss Strong about Chinese children.

"One of the Australian women in our group insists they are so clean, well-behaved, and reliable because they haven't got 'one bit of gumption' like Australian children," I said.

Miss Strong turned around in her chair, a battleship with guns blazing.

"The Chinese children have tremendous initiative," she charged. "They've certainly got more than the average American child who has no capacity for entertaining himself. Nor do you ever see them fight and shoving, or, for that matter, crying."

I had to admit that I had never seen a Chinese child squabbling with his peers ("Because everything belongs to everyone else," put in Miss Strong triumphantly), but I felt it was to remove the Chinese child from the realm of humanity by claiming that he is "never" unhappy while at the same time possessing "tremendous initiative."

Initiative is always costly, and this is especially true in a society where conformity of attitude to authority is one of the acid tests of belonging.

It was now twilight. Before leaving, I sent up another trial balloon. When Miss Strong mentioned she had once worked for the Hearst newspapers, I said I had too when I lived in the United States. In fact, they had asked me to do a series on China.

I was aware that Miss Strong lives in Peking under the grace and favor of the ever-vigilant regime and that the gist of our conversation sooner or later would be suitably deposited in the right pigeonhole. I had made up my mind, however, to tell Yu Shang-ven of an "offer" from the Hearst papers. How Miss Strong reacted to this little piece of intelligence would determine how and what I told him.

"Do the Chinese know?" she asked swiftly.

I said no, that it would have been detrimental to getting a visa. She smiled at this and said nothing.

I left in near darkness and decided to walk back to the hotel along the Chang An Boulevard. Its sidewalks are at least as wide as a four-lane freeway. On one a small crowd had gathered.

It was the sort of diversion that the Chinese love. A girl of about twenty, not pretty but with a broad and honest face and two childish looking pigtails, was clutching her bicycle. A man of about thirty-five, dressed in a bright navy sailcloth suit, held his, too. But he was haranguing and scolding the girl in the best tradition of Peking opera. A white-jacketed policeman came over and attempted to be conciliatory but the man would have none of it. Apparently the girl had rammed him with her bicycle. The crowd looked at the girl, then at the man, then back at the girl. The policeman gave up his futile efforts and stepped back into the crowd as a spectator.

It seemed interesting to me that in this so-called land of equality the girl said nothing, not one word in her own defense, but like Niobe, all tears, stood in red-faced silence, chin up, and took it all. Feeling that her humiliation would be greatly intensified by the knowledge that a foreigner was present, I moved away—after glaring ferociously at the man across the girl's shoulder. I could have been a unicorn for all he cared. I noticed the policeman looked a bit fidgety and tried to stop the verbal onslaught after he noticed me in the crowd. But the "injured party" simply shouted louder and continued his harangue.

I wondered if equality for women in China is much the same as it is in the West. There might be legal equality but psychological equality is another thing again. It exists, in the realities of daily life, only for those with either an independent bank account or, as a substitute, a profession. Mrs. Chia, I

119

felt, would have given the man with the bicycle a bit of old-fashioned what for.

Back at the hotel I had dinner. Then, in a meeting with Yu, I told him that the Hearst newspapers also had asked me to do a series of articles for them. I saw Yu pick up his ears at the sound of "Hearst" as Li translated it; then the answer came back:

"We are aware of the Hearst press, of William Randolph Hearst, Jr."

There was a minute's silence—during which I noted with surprise the fact that they had designated him "Jr." Then:

"We have no objections. We believe you will be fair and objective and we are grateful to you for being so sincere and open-hearted."

Two things struck me about Yu's reply. Assuming that he knew that I was on the staff of an American newspaper—a State Department official once told me that the Chinese Intelligence Service was "excellent"—his reply could only mean that they were not adverse to getting publicity, provided it was "objective."

Assuming that he didn't know, his decision was made with speed and decisiveness without consultation with anyone, although that most certainly followed. And he used simple, old-fashioned words: for a moment we spoke a common language.

This sense of communicating at a very fundamental level was to occur time and time again on the tour. Yet it was always brief, transient, and inevitably upsetting. For it would be there one moment and, without apparent reason or for only the slightest of reasons, gone the next, replaced by the usual impenetrable, abstract officialese. Our hosts were consistently polite, but I refer here to an intuitive communication beyond that, a communication whose presence or absence can best be sensed at times in silence.

There was one incident, however, when a Chinese official

—not one of the three in our group—was not polite. I would like to describe this incident because it points up not only my previous remarks about intuitive communication at a very fundamental, human level, but because it also added a little more weight to my over-all feeling that women in China, as elsewhere, have a way to go yet in gaining full equality.

The setting for the incident could not have been more idyllic. We were on one of the islands on Hangchow's exquisite West Lake, taken there in groups of twos and threes in a fleet of canopied boats rowed by silent, stolid-faced women. The pink lotus blossoms were so thick on one pond they all but covered the water: an arched bridge led to another where the density of golden carp had turned the water's surface to shimmering gold.

I was on the bridge when a broken lotus blossom, bruised and partially submerged, drifted by, the stem broken off. I stooped to pick it up. Before I could get off my knees the local Communist party official was at my side. I don't know what he said but his attitude reminded me of the angry "injured party" in Peking. He paused for a moment. Li Tieh-fei said briefly, quietly:

"Please put it back."

I said, holding out the broken reed in great surprise:

"It's broken off, half-dead, I was merely . . ."

"Put it back please."

Even before I could do it the party official started off again. He was a man of about thirty with a round face and excellent teeth: he smiled a lot. Now he was shouting a lot, looking, in his high-necked gray tunic, the perfect picture of the neurotically compulsive bureaucrat. His agitation was most heartfelt: only training, I felt, was stopping him from seizing the blossom from my hands and putting it back in the lake.

I put the flower back, got off my knees, and walked away,

not daring to trust myself to speak: as I moved, I could hear Li giving a swift translation of the official's speech:

"We teach the children of China to take care of beautiful things. We are all responsible for keeping our country beautiful. This is fundamentally correct. A child might see you touching a flower. It would be a shocking scandal to them, a bad example. . . ."

"Take it easy, Lisa," one of the Australian men said. "It's all a lot of bloody nonsense."

We were still walking in the gardens a half hour later when Li and the party official approached. Again the party official made a speech but this time it was brief and conciliatory.

"He says, Mrs. Hobbs, that he wants you to know he was only joking earlier," said Li.

"What rot!" The words sprang to my lips but I held them back in a flash second of doubt. Is it possible that he was only joking? I hesitated—a fatal mistake under the circumstances —and discretion took over as the better part of valor. I turned: I would teach him some manners Western style!

"It is good," I said in the most noncommittal tone I could voice, "to teach your children to love beautiful things."

He looked at me keenly. Did he think I believed his excuse that he was joking? I believe so, for soon his impeccable smile was at work again.

Going back to our little canopied canoes—we called them "the royal barges"—I noticed that Yu and Li were both tense and silent. They spoke neither to one another nor to me, but helped me into the boat, fussed over my comfort, and Yu even asked if he could sit next to me! They had looked after us with such care and now this had to happen! Back on the other side, I said to Li quietly, making no attempt to disguise my anger:

122

"I must have been mad not saying what I really thought: now I'm more burned at myself than I am at him!"

Li looked at me—and I had no doubt that he felt exactly the same way. Neither he nor Yu said one word but I realized too late, if with some gratification, that both of them would have felt justice well served if I had raised a little hell of my own on the island with the lotus blossoms.

11

If a stranger came
to the United States and visited six large cities hundreds of miles apart, stopping at small towns en route from one city to another, would he be able to make a valid judgment as to whether or not the people of the United States were getting enough to eat?

That was my situation in China and that was the question I wanted to answer.

In the United States, with its fleets of mammoth intercontinental trucks moving on a network of coast-to-coast and border-to-border highways, day and night; with commercial aircraft visible overhead every hour of the day and the freight sections of those airports open to the public and operating at full capacity; with an interlacing of freight trains connecting city to city and town to town—I believe it would be valid to make a judgment on the food situation in the entire country on the basis of a trip such as mine.

The situation in China is vastly different. Large expanses of that vast land are virtually isolated. Roads are scarce and often in bad repair. Air freight, as it is known in the United

124

States, barely exists. By official admission, the marketing problems of the rural areas are gross; it is not unreasonable to assume that marketing problems in the rural areas result in both surpluses and shortages.

No tourist in China is free to wander at will from city to city to investigate for himself. All tourist groups follow a package tour arranged by Luxingshe. Thirty such tours are offered, varying only in the number of cities visited and the length of stay. The shortest tour is one of eight days and the longest twenty-six. Only nine cities are open to tourists: of those we did not visit—Tientsin, Nanking, and Wuhan. Tourists who aren't traveling with a group, such as the Canadian farmer and his wife, or the English secretary that we met in Shanghai, can do their actual traveling from city to city alone, but they are put on the plane or train by an interpreter or Luxingshe official and are met at the other end by an interpreter or guide. Even when alone, however, the visitor can't deviate from the "open" city route.

In those six cities that I visited, and in the rural areas surrounding those cities, I saw no evidence of any food shortage. However, because of China's size—roughly 90,000 square miles larger than the United States—and because of her marketing problems, any assumption that the conditions I saw were identical with those in many other, unseen cities would be rash. Conditions in the unseen cities could have been better or they could have been worse. Nonetheless, the cities that we did visit, although in the eastern part only, were separated from each other by hundreds of miles.

The Chinese are not eating luxuriously and their diet might well be tedious but they are eating adequately. How do I know? I looked at the people. In the market places, in the nurseries, in the parks—whenever a baby was presented to me I checked the scalp, the nails, the gait of growing legs; in the shower rooms of the communes the girls and young women gave proof positive that the bulge in the rough working suit was not cotton padding; when students shook my hand I held on for as long as I decently could, taking in the condition of teeth, the state of the skin, the brightness of the eye. With the children I was particularly concerned; but the legs were straight, the hair thick and glossy, the nails neatly clipped, not split and broken off, and the teeth incredibly white and polished. The teeth of the elderly were invariably bad—a half-dozen scattered stumps. But as for rickets or malnutrition, I couldn't turn up one case.

Secondly, I poked around down the back alleys and off the side streets. In the cities, half the rooms that comprise "home" open onto the sidewalk. When the city slowed down to eat at twilight, I looked in to see what was on the table in countless such rooms. There always appeared to be enough.

Sometimes I wasn't too welcome. It would take a minute or two of staring to get used to the gloom, but when I did often as not this was what I saw: one or two older people, a younger couple and two children, and perhaps a baby next to the mother, a large bowl of steaming rice in the center of a table at floor level, a bowl of steaming greens in some sort of sticky colorless sauce, and sometimes a piece of fish or maybe an egg mix in a smaller bowl. Not everyone had the latter items. Everyone squatted around shoveling the food in with brusque flips of their chopsticks. The only remnants left were a few grains of rice sticking to the bowls, but if there was no surplus there was no starvation either. Nor did I ever hear children cry fretfully, as they can be heard night and day in India when the food is gone and hunger remains.

I also went to the markets, a score of them and hundreds of miles apart, and watched what the housewives of China are bringing home to the family pantry. I had no way of knowing whether the women were buying for a day or a week. As the

Chinese traditionally shop every day, and as nobody has refrigerators, it is reasonable to assume the purchases covered a couple of days at most.

The market stalls were laden with produce. There were plenty of fresh green vegetables, potatoes, eggs, fish, pork, and poultry. I saw no beef or lamb for sale. Eggs cost 60 Chinese cents a half kilo—which is about 30 U.S. cents a pound. It was not uncommon to see a housewife buy a dozen or two eggs. French green beans (and the quality was good) cost 7 U.S. cents a pound. Poor quality potatoes sold at 10 U.S. cents a pound, good ones at 11 cents.

The price of duck ranged up from 47 U.S. cents a pound for the roasted product, 38 U.S. cents uncooked. Pork was about 54 U.S. cents a pound, while fresh fish sold from 25 U.S. cents a pound to 18 U.S. cents for salted fish.

Rice—here my notes fail me completely with the mere notation "cheap"—is rationed according to occupation. China has no grain surfeit, as is evidenced by the fact that she purchased this year's entire wheat crop from Australia—120,200,-000 tons valued at $115,000,000 and, on October 27, 1965, contracted with the Canadian Wheat Board to buy $403,000,-000 worth of wheat over the next three years. China is engaged in a program to educate the people away from rice and onto wheat, so far a rather futile task. The purchase of this wheat from Australia, by the way, resulted in two different strains of speculation in rumor-rife Hong Kong—that she was storing it in underground silos in case of war, or that it was an economically shrewd move to export her high-priced grains for lower-priced imported wheat.

As cheap as food is by our standards it still looms fairly large when measured against wages. It is the major living expense way above any other item. This brings me to the question of wages and, more generally, working conditions in the roaring mills and belching factories that, in an economy that has weeded out personal consumer services, provide the great bulk of employment for city workers.

Textile Mill Number Two in Peking appeared to be typical, in wages, atmosphere, rules and regulations, and upward mobility, of the dozen factories I visited. For instance, when we arrived, we were greeted by traditional Chinese music piped from loudspeakers at the side of the main door. In the bitumen yard before the building, scores of young girls, just coming off the night shift, were doing the half hour of folk dancing required before being allowed to go home. The tune, a lively jig with traditional Chinese instruments, was about the joy of being able to help one's country. The girls stopped when they saw us to clap their traditional greeting; then, cheeks flushed and looking a bit overheated—they were all wearing padded jackets—they were off again, kicking and twirling and facing their partners. I did a few turns with the girls—not only as a friendly gesture but because folk dancing offers one of the few opportunities of kicking up one's heels in today's China.

There was nothing novel about this dancing session: all workers in China must do daily exercise of one kind or another—dancing, *tai chi chuan*, or more vigorous calisthenics. During any hour of the day it's possible to see students or typists or factory workers or railway station keepers lining up for their daily dozen. There is no choice; unless they are sick they must join in. Doctors and nurses at hospitals aren't excused, although with the more prestigious professions the exercises can be done individually.

After our little fling we went into the administrative building to meet the director, Madame Kao Ya, who sat us down, inevitably, to tea.

Madame Kao was a typical woman factory director—middle-aged, polite and intense, no make-up, vestiges of a

128

permanent wave, stockily built, wearing a tailored beige jacket and slacks, and addicted to the stereotyped phrasing that most official Chinese women appear to relish.

The average age of the workers, she said, was twenty-seven. Most of them lived opposite the factory in a massive apartment complex: they earned an average monthly wage of 60 yuan (about $30). The minimum wage was 40 yuan ($20) and the highest 100 yuan, workers being paid according to their ability. Apprentices, starting at eighteen years, earned 30 yuan.

Madame Kao said she and the chief engineer (a woman who was present at the meeting) each drew 150 yuan ($75). Raises, she said, were decided by the work teams themselves and not by the leadership.

I questioned the practicality of a system wherein a group of young girls would be responsible for the picking and choosing of raises for their teammates.

"Such a system is only possible in socialism," she replied through interpreter Li. "It is to each team's credit that production be raised. They are glad to see a member become more productive. For instance, the first shift is always thinking about better conditions for the next shift. They get everything ready: the spirit of mutual help is promoted.

"How have we been able to do this?" Madame Kao asked in a flat voice, leading up to the old punch line. "We have studied Chairman Mao's thinking and have been able to overcome our difficulties. Every year we have overfulfilled the state target. In some products the quality is not very high. How shall we raise it? We have launched a campaign to improve quality by studying the works of Chairman Mao."

The concept of reading political works to upgrade production standards had seemed a lot of bunk to me before I went to China. I could see "strength-through-joy" programs whipping up enthusiasm and investing the worker with both energy and ambition. This would increase productivity, but for the life of me I couldn't see how it could upgrade quality, nor make hens lay more eggs, or fields grow more grain, or make silk softer or cotton finer. I came to see, however, that the apparently simple-minded slogans are a deceptively powerful force, a philosophy promulgated in a verbal shorthand.

Two factors explain the sense of upward thrust that this sloganeering has managed to engender. One is constant and skillful repetition by every means of communication—public address systems in the carriages of trains, popular songs to which the factory hands danced, banners on the classroom walls—until entire conversations are strung together by phrases, slogans, catch-cries. The second factor responsible for the effectiveness of the slogans has been that they are directly connected to actual experiences that the people undergo: they are not ephemeral aspirations, they are words that the worker's fingers can translate into direct action. Madame Kao's remarks about studying Mao's works was not just propagandistic chatter.

All workers must give some of their spare time to studying politics. A certain number of lectures and discussion groups must be attended monthly. At all these discussions, the overriding theme is the idea of working, not for private gain, but for the benefit of all society. The value of the individual's contribution is constantly emphasized: without doubt, it results in the worker identifying himself with an important and worthwhile goal, regardless of the menial nature of his offering.

"Dare to think and dare to do" is one of Mao Tse-tung's most quoted admonitions. Its constant repetition is one of the many means employed to pick up minds turned toward the Middle Ages and turn them around to face the twentieth century. Men and women who would never have conceived of trying to change anything in the factory or on the farm are

130

encouraged to innovate. Their sense of value, of importance, is undoubtedly bolstered by the results of another admonition, "Theory must be combined with practice." This, wisely or otherwise, has brought the scientist, professor, and surgeon onto the communes and into the factories to labor for two weeks a year, while the laborer becomes their master apprentice for that period. At the same time, the laborer is exposed —for the first time perhaps—to the realm of the classroom in part-time or evening classes.

Genuine technical innovations appear to have been the result in the factories. In a Soochow silk factory we met a young woman of thirty, looking years younger than that with her white cap stuck at a gamine angle at the back of her head. The male factory director told us that she had invented a new method of feeding the fine silk strand into the loom. I couldn't understand the technicalities but apparently it speeded the process up and reduced breakage of the fragile strands. Breakage of the strands, constantly responsible for shutting off one loom while it was repaired, had been eliminated. In Madame Kao's textile mill we were told that the layout of the room into which the cotton bales were delivered had been completely revamped to increase efficiency following suggestions made by the workers in that room. In one rural classroom, which lacked any textbooks or exercise books, I saw an enthusiastic young man teaching lads of about eight some of the principles of geometry by making them fold cut-up newspapers.

This spirit of innovation is encouraged just as strongly on the farms as in the factories. By doing such things as building their own fertilizer factory—described earlier in the chapter on the Vietnamese Friendship Commune—younger farm workers and government technical advisers have opened up an entirely new world to the older farmers of China. Before, they had never heard of artificial fertilizer; now they themselves

131

have participated in its manufacture! They might not be sure of how it works but the improved grain crop proves it does! Through compulsory night classes, they have also been taught the value of hygiene—that it is profitable to clean the pig pens better, to remove the sick hen from the coop. The goal has obviously been to give the meanest peasant the idea that he is a man who matters, whose tasks have meaning and value. Believing this, he works harder, and all society benefits. The granting of a small private plot to each communal family provides the farmer with what is, to every peasant, meaningful evidence of upward mobility. Such grants could also well be an oblique acknowledgment by Peking that the need to possess personal property is, regardless of Marxism-Leninism, inherent in all mankind.

Observing that all the plots appeared to be of equal value or size, I found that their location is decided by communal discussion. A man who works a hillside, for instance, will get a larger area than a man who has his plot in a rich little culvert. A man whose plot is conveniently situated near water might be allowed a larger plot if he allows a path to cross his field.

There is, of course, a definite limit on the contribution that simple technical innovations and cleaner pig pens can make to a country's economy, but China is far from reaching that point at this time.

All these things Madame Kao touched on unwittingly when she spoke of her girls upgrading quality, as well as quantity, by reading the works of Chairman Mao. She then took us through the well-lit factory. In one section the noise was deafening. I asked if the workers were allowed to leave for a minute or two every hour or so, but was told they had a regular eight-hour shift in this section as anywhere else. I remarked that continuous exposure to such noise would eventually damage the hearing capacity but my remark was received in silence. I asked if the girls received extra pay and was told no.

Fortunately, this section was almost entirely automatic: there was no more than a handful of girls in the vast hell of noise. They walked from one machine to another, checking, peering, serious, and efficient: we couldn't get out of the intolerable noise quickly enough.

Passing through one large section, I noticed that there were no workers and the looms were idle. I was told, on enquiry, that the workers were all at lunch. I don't think Madame Kao appreciated my questions: she ran a tight ship, one felt, and it was none of my business. Her explanation was one of the very few nonpolitical remarks or explanations given that I couldn't accept. I could not tell whether the machines had been used recently or not: but there were no banners or slogans to be seen—and that, more surely than anything, meant that no workers were operating in this end of the factory. I wondered at Madame Kao's judgment in making a statement so obviously open to question: perhaps she did not feel she owed me any explanation. With cotton rationed to 7 yards per person a year, I concluded the looms were idle because of a shortage of raw material.

In another section of the huge factory was a red banner reading:

"Study Chairman Mao's work well in order to raise our quality."

Underneath was a blackboard for general notices. It was empty, however, except for a sketched bouquet of flowers in colorful chalk and a scroll-like notice:

"Welcome to our foreign guests."

The young girls, in white overalls and their long hair tucked under visored caps, looked contented enough. Those who were working where the fiber was teased wore white masks over their nose and mouth to keep the fine hairs out of their lungs. The sight of a white facial mask, introduced by the Japanese Occupation forces, is now common in China.

They are regarded as a scientific way of stopping the dissemination of cold germs. People wear them on the streets, in offices and shops and schools. Mothers seem to be particularly fond of them, popping them on the snuffling noses of their toddlers by the hundreds. They are tied at the back of the head just like surgical masks. The idea of blowing and breathing into a mask that undoubtedly dampens with saliva as the day goes on seemed to me like a good idea for spreading germs. The main value of this idea in China, however, has probably been the exposure of millions of people to the realization that disease is spread by bugs too small to see.

These young girls worked side by side with the men, who sometimes wore overalls, sometimes just shorts and T-shirts. There was an easy air of camaraderie between the sexes.

When we were through with the factory, Madame Kao took us across the boulevard to the block apartments. These were very similar to public housing anywhere, except perhaps for the avenues dividing the various sections. These were heavily planted with trees and often as not with a center dividing strip of shrubs and plants. There were children playing everywhere, and an air of business as the girls on free time strolled along in groups chatting while others hurried to the central dining room.

Inside, we were shown the rooms in which the workers lived. Each family had one room about 12 by 14 feet. They were all steam heated, had electricity, and the kitchen was supplied with butane gas. The kitchen, about the size of an American bathroom, and the bathroom and separate toilet, were shared by three or four families.

Rent, which included utilities, costs 50 U.S. cents a month for a single person. In comparison, a pack of cigarettes in China costs 20 U.S. cents. Married couples paid 2 yuan ($1) a month. Couples could either eat at home or pay 12–15 yuan ($6–$7.50) a month for three meals a day in the communal dining room. This huge hall, with cafeteria-style service and inexpensive wooden tables and chairs, was serving eight different dishes, plus rice, and four different sorts of bread the day we visited. The tables were small, holding about six persons, and there was a lot of noise, smoking, and laughter. The counters were wooden and the food served into wooden bowls from large vats. The workers all took rice and one other dish. We were asked behind the counter into the back section where six cooks in white and about half a dozen girls were rolling and kneading dough and slicing something that looked like corn bread into fair-sized hunks.

Australians are very informal: everyone immediately started sampling everything. We were hustled out in no time: I think our Chinese hosts were quite shocked by our behavior!

There was a central barber shop used by both men and women, where a haircut could be had for 8 U.S. cents—almost the same as a week's rent for a single person! It was as busy as a market—shaving, cutting, clipping, permanent waving (for the women, of course), all at once.

There seemed little evidence in the apartments of the purchase of nonessential goods. I asked Madame Kao what higher paid workers did with their extra money.

Radios, she said, were a popular purchase. These cost from 50–150 yuan ($25–$75). Bicycles, the only method of city transportation other than a bus, cost from 150–200 yuan ($75–$100). Later, I checked these prices in a Peking department store and found them to be accurate.

The girls' most popular acquisition was a sewing machine, which cost 140 yuan ($70).

"When they are single," said Madame Kao, "they buy their clothes at the store. But," she added, hitting a familiar note, "when they marry they make them themselves."

A tiny, elderly lady in black hovered in the hall. She wore a glossy black bun and displayed several golden teeth. I told a

135

translator I'd like to see her room. We had a nice visit together.

She told me her rent was 2 yuan ($1) a month: she had retired from her factory job on a pension of 36 yuan ($18) a month, which was based on 70 per cent of her earnings prior to retirement. She was very lively and obviously enormously proud of her home. In particular, she could barely hide her feelings over her latest acquisition—two modern upholstered armchairs on either side of a small coffee table.

"I bought the whole set for 76 yuan," she said, and even though I didn't understand Chinese the incredulity—that she could buy such riches—came through and was confirmed by her wrinkled smile.

On the wall was a picture of Chairman Mao Tse-tung. She pointed to it and beamed. Well, you couldn't blame her: he had done her proud!

Schools for the workers' children were a little distance down the tree-lined walk, where the dirt had been tamped into concrete firmness.

The first graders were doing a dance—*The Planting of the Grapes*. Another group, coming out of the two-story school building, ran into us and spontaneously clapped and shouted, "Good morning, Uncles and Aunties." Upstairs, the fat little toddlers—the girls wearing their hair caught by a rubber band in a thin, little topknot on the crown of their heads—were singing for us with marked enthusiasm: *Shuh whei tuyi hao*.

"What's that?" I asked.

"It means, socialism is good."

They looked barely old enough to talk.

The next morning, for the first and only time during my China visit, the telephone in my bedroom rang.

"Is that Mrs. Hobbs?"

"Yes...." The voice was that of an American: my heart flipped over. "Who is this?"

136

"This is Anna Louise Strong."

"Oh, Miss Strong..." I said in comprehending relief. "How are you?"

"Mrs. Hobbs." The voice was firm but kindly. "I feel there are a few things about our conversation that I wish to clarify."

For a few minutes Miss Strong spoke about her opinions on the Sino-Soviet split, coexistence and one or two other subjects that we had touched on but never really discussed. Then she said something like:

"You must speak to them, Mrs. Hobbs. It's up to you, of course."

I said nothing. I didn't know what to say. I felt it extremely unlikely that I would receive a telephone call in Peking from anyone without it being bugged. But I was by no means sure that Miss Strong, a shrewd and experienced ex-newspaperwoman herself, hadn't guessed the whole truth.

"You are referring to the offer I received from the Hearst organization?"

"Yes I am, Mrs. Hobbs. It would be better to be open about it."

I told her that I had already deposited the matter in Mr. Yu's hands and that he had told me there would be no objection. She sounded gratified at that and said I had done the right thing.

"Maybe I'm really beginning to think 'correctly,'" I said by way of a joke.

But if Miss Strong chuckled the telephone didn't catch it.

We said goodbye to one another politely and hung up.

12

It was curious that

I was to spend my last day in Peking out of touch, as it were, with this century. Luxingshe had arranged that those of us who wished could go to the Great Wall and the Ming Tombs —all in one glorious day. It was to provide a sharp and welcome reminder of the fact that whatever is happening in China today is happening within the periphery of a culture that was far advanced when the United States was still uninhabited.

There is an old saying about the streets of Peking and its environs:

When there is no wind there is three feet of dust;
When there is rain the whole street is mud.

Those who have made the trip to the Wall before Liberation—an hour's train trip from Peking to the Green Dragon Bridge and then half an hour's walk—would find the excursion I made greatly different. A road, paved but for the last final, winding stages, leads from downtown Peking to the shadow of the great gray Wall itself.

It sits there like a dragon, twisting and turning through gorges, running along the ridges of the steep, rocky hills that ripple sharply until they terminate in great, jagged mountains. And here the Wall disappears again, continuing on its incredible 1,700-mile course. It is said that if the Wall were straightened out, its loops and meanderings pushed into line, it would run some 2,500 miles. It follows, instead, the line of least resistance, avoiding gullies and chasms and clinging to the ridge like some great, gray leech, from Linyu in northeast China to the frontiers of Tibet.

Mrs. Chia, with us to interpret, said she had been there a week earlier and it was covered with snow. On our visit it was bitterly cold—no snow but fog swept down from the mountains, sucked in through Nan K'ou Pass, just as white and just as damp. I wanted to walk alone along the Wall's broad parapet in solitude, but its incline is somewhat steep and the gray stones that make up its surface are slippery and treacherous. A Communist party official, in his gray outfit, stayed at my side. He was a kindly man, perhaps forty, serious and quiet. He looked more Occidental than Oriental. He spoke no English, but everything betrayed his anxiety that I might slip. The Chinese are good at silence: it isn't uncomfortable as it is so often in the West. I welcomed the silence and savored the situation with its unique suggestion of history encapsuled—a walk along the 2,100-year-old Wall and a Marxist-Leninist to catch me if I came a cropper.

Then on to the Ming Tombs, driving back through Nan K'ou, passing about halfway the village of Chuyungkuan. The Language Arch there, dated 1345, with Buddhist figures and symbols, bears inscriptions in Chinese, Mongolian, Uigur, Tibetan, Sanskrit, and Tangut, and has been a mecca for archaeologists for centuries.

I walked to the fringe of the ancient village. The mud bricks of many houses had crumbled into a pile of yellow

139

dust. The main street was of gray stone set into the soil: no lichens or weeds broke through the cracks. The village seemed barren, as if the very soil which once gave the village life had shrunk and become sterile with the passage of time. I thought the village was deserted but a tall, thin, middle-aged woman in black stepped out from one of the open doorways on the main street. Her eyes swept by me without acknowledgment and she went off in her black cloth shoes toward the other side of the village. There were no animals: the silence was absolute. To the north, the stony ground of the village fell away to a gully and then swept up into the mountains. Through the mist, a segment of the Great Wall was visible.

Looking back to the parapet of the old fort on the extremity of the village, I could see Yu standing, watching me. I waved and walked on. Something was alive: here fruit blossom was in hectic strawberry-colored bloom. Standing near the arch, however, was something that could have been as old as the Wall—a round table of stone, about 3 feet high, the top of which was worn into a bowl a couple of inches deep by a smooth, rolling stone which, even now, lay idle in the center. Obviously, it was where the villagers had crushed their grain, and by its round, silken smooth lines, had done so for many years. It was timeless and quite beautiful: I took a picture of it. But somehow I had a feeling that Yu, who was by now standing nearby, didn't like my photographing it.

A few days later I was to be told by an interpreter, ostensibly out of the blue and in casual conversation:

"Some people, pretending to be friends, come here and specialize in taking pictures of poor people and poor conditions, as if there had been no improvements, as if we had accomplished nothing. These pictures have been used abroad to ridicule us. We know we are backward in many ways but we do ask that you be fair and take the good with the bad."

140

This worry that I was taking "backward" pictures was probably in Yu's mind when I photographed the grinder: it was a fear that grew measurably as my visit progressed. Certainly, it is unlikely that he could perceive the grinder as an object of aesthetic interest: as a child, he had lived in such a village with such equipment and had almost starved. I must say that in spite of his anxiety, no restrictions were ever placed on my photography. There is, in fact, a customs regulation in China that no unexposed film can leave the country. It is rarely invoked: in my case, the authorities would have been more than justified in making use of it. Instead, I left with twenty rolls of unexposed color film.

This question of what was historically and aesthetically interesting to the tourist was often at variance with, and a matter of great perplexity to, our guides. For instance, we spent a whole morning in Peking at the Museum of Modern Art but could not find time to stop at the Kuan Hsian T'ai (Astronomical Observatory) on our way there. We passed the internationally famous, 300-year-old station, with its weird and extraordinary instruments pointing accusingly at the sky, like a display of avant-garde sculpture, to rush to the museum where a collection of propaganda posters and cartoons of little interest awaited us. Incidentally, a large number of these cartoons dealt with America's role in airlifting European nationals out of the Congo when hostilities threatened their lives. The most popular representation of America was as a huge snake, split tongue licking the air while its body crushed the peoples of Africa. All pieces in the museum supposedly were done by farm and factory workers, and hang in the museum because of their special "merit."

By now our bus was entering the basin-shaped, 3½-mile area which contains thirteen imperial Ming tombs. It was an excursion that was to prove every bit as splendid as a visit to Egypt's pyramids. To the east, west, and north, the basin

141

is screened by mountain ridges while to the south there is a pass, flanked by the Dragon and Tiger Mountains, that opens onto the desolate flats known as the Peking Plains.

Chia said that great efforts in restoration and historical research had been made on this site in the past ten years. The area was a base for guerrilla activities during the Japanese occupation and until 1956 no regime had had either the money or the interest to investigate properly, and adequately protect this repository of historic and cultural treasures.

"Some of the tombs were popular tourist spots years ago," said Chia. But the existence of Emperor Wan Li's Underground Palace tomb was suspected but not confirmed until about 1957.

At this time an intensive archaeological study was undertaken.

"The diggings had to proceed with tremendous caution. After the tombs had been completed in the early seventeenth century, the slaves were shot, probably with arrows, to prevent the location of the tombs being disclosed. Then, technical experts took over and planted booby traps and land mines into the sides of the stone walls. The tunnels were walled over in stone, of course, and anyone attempting to find it ran the danger of setting off a trap."

Chia said that she had heard that some of the steel traps were set off during the search and even a few mines detonated, but she didn't know if this was a fact or not.

The first structure that came into view in this isolated area was a marble archway, sitting up straight like the ornate towers that sit white and fragile on the top of a wedding cake. A little dust blew across the plain; the road ran through the archway like a ribbon.

Now the road swept into the Alley of the Animals. For over a mile, spaced neatly apart, twenty-four stone beasts and twelve statues of men stand watch over the road of the final

142

journey. About 10 feet tall, and perfectly proportioned, there are four each of lions, unicorns, camels, elephants, horses, and *chi lin*, a mythical beast; the twelve men represent four military officers, four civil officers and four officers of "merit" (special appointments for outstanding service to the Emperor or Empress).

Some idea of the progress that China has made in developing its historic sites, both for the pleasure of its own people and as a tourist draw, can be gleaned from this passage taken from a guide to Peking, written and published there only months before Liberation. A visit to the tombs can take one day, the author, an Englishwoman, warns. It can be made by a car in three hours or by taking a train to Nan K'ou and then a "donkey for the 7 miles' trip."

Now we passed what is considered by art experts, Occidental and Oriental, to be the most beautiful Pai Lou in China. Built in 1541, the Ta Hung Men (Great Red Gate) seems to grow out of the dusty prairie like Chinese ideographs that have sprung to solid life. The Pai Lou is an archway put up solely for decorative purposes like Rome's Arch of Constantine: they are to be seen, in carved and painted wood, spanning the humblest city streets. The Ta Hung Men, built in marble, has five archways, those on the outside being lowest, that in the center being highest. The bases of the massive pillars were set into highly ornamental blocks: the pillars shot up into a roof of glazed and crimson tiles. At the near base of each pillar, crouching on the ornamental blocks, was a lion, eyes toward the center archway through which, in times long gone, the scent of incense, the clashing of gongs, and the masked and glittering cortege of royal mourners passed.

What an imagination Emperor Yung Lo had! Rumor says he picked the area because of his unpopularity in Nanking, where royalty was usually buried. This was in 1409: his choice set a precedent that was followed by twelve other Ming emperors and their queens. Yung Lo did not build the Ta Hung Men—that was erected about a century after his death —but he didn't remain idle after picking out his burial plot. His grandiose funeral plans were followed by an even more ambitious project—the building up and beautification of Peking into a major capital. The general layout that he chose is that of Peking today.

With our bus parked now, we walked through the ornate red and gold livery of the Dragon and Phoenix Gates. Now the great sacrificial hall was visible. Meant to honor the Emperors, it remains instead more of a monument to those coolies who shed their sweat and blood to bring the Ming Emperors' grandiose dreams to reality. In this, and in its size and grandeur, the hall reflects the same spirit that created the Egyptian pyramids but was, to my mind, much richer both in conception and execution.

The hall stands on a three-tiered white stone foundation. From the base spring forth long-necked dragon-like gargoyles that reminded me of those on the pyramids of Teotihuacán outside Mexico City. Inside are forty massive teakwood pillars: when three of us linked arms we could not ring their girth. The transportation of these monstrous trees from the remote areas of South China during the sixteenth century, when the hall was built, must have been like that of the stones for the pyramids of Egypt, on a sea of human sweat.

Passing out of the hall we walked up the gently sloping pine- and cyprus-dotted hill under which the tomb, or Underground Palace, of the Emperor Wan Li is located. Chia said we were visiting this tomb, the most recently excavated, rather than that of founder Yung Lo, on which restoration work was presently being done. On top of the hill a small structure has been erected to protect the entrance to the tomb—now reshaped into seven flights of concrete stairway.

Now I felt I had entered the womb of China, for the very air stank with a smothering sense of fecund time. Wan Li had not built himself a tomb: it was indeed a palace underground.

The palace comprised five large chambers, each with a ceiling of about 20 feet. The main hall can be envisioned as forming the vertical stroke of the letter T. The actual burial chamber at the back of it formed the cross stroke. There were two rooms to each side of the letter T and an entrance chamber into one of them at the bottom of the flight of stairs. These two chambers that led into the main hall were perhaps 30 by 20 feet: the connecting doors were each made of one solid piece of marble. There were no columns or supporting beams anywhere.

In the main hall, about 50 feet long and 20 feet wide, three marble thrones stood erect in empty, lonely splendor. The centuries had rubbed the sweeping, simple lines of their curved arms and plain, ramrod back into a rich patina. Standing before them, as if still offering mute and dogged tribute, was a porcelain vase, rounded and waist-high. It was in this that the sesame oil was burned after burial. The Everlasting Lamp, as the guides designated it, was still half-filled with oil and the wick only partially burned, when the tomb had been opened.

At the back of this room was the actual tomb. Here, three large coffins lay side by side on a stone platform raised a foot off the concrete floor. The center coffin, large and crimson-painted, contained the Emperor's body; to his left, the body of his first empress, Hsiao Tuan, had been placed; to his right the second empress, Hsiao Ching. The coffins which contained the bodies had then been placed in a larger, almost square, outer coffin. Entrance into this tomb room was through a massive door cast in bronze. It staggered the imagination to think of the human energy spent both in its creation and transportation here.

When the tomb was opened, articles of incredible craftsmanship and luxury had been found here—porcelain, jade belts, rings, a crown of pure gold, the most intricate headdresses, bowls of gold, and much jewelry of precious and semiprecious stones. We saw some of the treasure in a well-designed museum that now adjoins this tomb site.

On the way back from the tombs, I found myself seated next to Mrs. Chia. She asked me what I liked most about Peking. I replied promptly that, it might seem a foolish thing, but the absence of heavy motor traffic was a most attractive feature.

"You should see cities like New York and Sydney during rush hours," I said, "traffic bumper to bumper and people locked behind the steering wheels, unable to get out of it."

"Yes," she said with animation, "I have heard of this. It is not a problem we have to worry about—not for some time, anyway," she threw in.

We both fell silent with our own thoughts. Finally I decided to broach another subject:

"What problems would a woman here have to worry about? Her husband has secured employment: she has too. Sick leave is provided for, illness paid for by the state. All of society supports mothers in their attempt to teach children manners and ethical behavior. What problems would a woman have? Do you have friends, do you visit one another's homes?"

Chia (we called her "Mrs." only sometimes, "Mr." and "Mrs." having no meaning in Chinese) was silent and I wondered if I had gone too far. The Chinese are jealous of their privacy.

After a few moments she said quietly:

"Of course we have friends, just like everyone else. For in-

146

stance, we make friends at the university who become lifelong friends. We visit each others' homes. When we have difficulties we speak our hearts to each other."

I sensed I was on very delicate ground, yet my curiosity was eating me alive.

"But what sort of difficulties?" I persisted.

"Well ..." she thought for a minute and then said seriously and circumspectly: "A young girl and a young man might like each other very much. They think perhaps they will get married. But then, there's a difference of opinion over this or that, and they have a quarrel. These things happen here just like everywhere else." She added with a smile:

"People who are fond of each other can often find lots of things to quarrel about."

Gathering my courage, I broached the subject of the attitude of Chinese women toward sex. Chia looked so serious that I apologized but said I could hardly ask Yu for such information. At this she smiled and said she understood this subject was of enormous interest to the West, particularly America.

"I understand that articles and books are written about it, as if it were a subject separate from the rest of life. Is this true then?" She wrinkled her pale face and looked perplexed. "It is very different here. We do not discuss it: a woman would not talk about it even to a group of friends, never even to a close friend."

Chia, the mother of two children, said that the Chinese married woman doesn't conceive of sex either as a pleasure or a duty.

"She doesn't think of it as separate from everything else: it is just a part of the whole. When most of us think of marriage, I think it is about our home and children most of all. The welfare of the children, the responsibility of raising them, really takes first place."

147

But what if the couple simply don't get on and are miserably unhappy?

"Married people can always get a divorce," she said. "It is not difficult. However, it is only in recent years that women have had a free choice of husbands. Formerly the husband was picked by the parents and the bride didn't see him until the wedding day. Now the young girls are taught that they have both a privilege and a responsibility with their free choice. Making their decision freely, they should stick with it if humanly possible."

"Who usually gets the children if a couple divorce?" I asked.

"If there are small children, then there might be some difficulty getting a divorce," Chia said. "If the marriage just won't work they can probably get one, but they must try very hard first to make it work out. Then, if the court thinks a divorce is justified, the mother usually gets the children and the father must contribute to their support. There is very little divorce, however."

I was then asked if I considered sex to be the most important part of marriage. I replied only that it was a part of marriage in which couples must reach a mutual understanding. If they could not understand one another's attitudes and needs in this area, then tension spread throughout the entire relationship. She nodded at this, as if to say, that is true even in China!

I then asked Chia about premarital behavior, remarking that only twice did I see couples holding hands or walking arm in arm. She made this observation:

"The young people have been taught what we call 'Communist morality.' They are never flippant toward marriage. The thought of premarital sex is truly shocking. Once a couple decide to marry, a man will kiss his girl, but perhaps only once or twice before marriage. We don't relate a great show of affection with depth of feeling."

I think this observation is a cocktail of truth, personal feeling, and unwitting propaganda. The Chinese struck me as being people of great passion and depth. I am sure they are never flippant toward marriage: on the other hand I think it removes Chinese men from the realm of mankind to think that they think or feel any differently toward their sweethearts than men of other races. I doubt very much indeed that the Chinese act their feelings out as freely as Western bachelors do, especially now when their whole society is geared to a utilitarian, hard-working, disciplined, almost monastic sort of existence. Premarital sex might be held as unethical, undesirable, unwise for a variety of reasons, but I doubt that the notion would be considered "shocking," at least among the men.

As for birth control:

"Contraceptives are extremely cheap—just a few cents—and can be purchased almost anywhere. We have a large campaign going to teach the people the necessity of limiting their families. More and more women realize that our living standards can only be realized in this way."

Later, on our return to Canton, I was to see part of this drive for planned parenthood at a birth control exhibition in the People's Cultural Park. It was interesting to see couples, who in all don't kiss more than a few times before marriage, surveying the exhibit with a deep, impersonal interest. It seemed to bear out Chia's contention that sex, as such, is not divorced from the realities of everyday living. The exhibition included all the mechanical devices employed in the West. A large black and white picture showed a young couple with two children receiving a special award from a government official in recognition of the example they had set for other factory workers by having only two children. The picture showed the smiling group before a bungalow-type house and a printed notice indicated that all of China will eventually prosper likewise if the population growth is curtailed.

Can anyone buy contraceptives, I asked Chia; teenagers perhaps?

"Yes, but not young people, of course. They would have no need. There is a legal age for marriage: if the shopkeeper wanted to he could ask for some identification but I assure you this is not necessary. Your question hardly makes sense in China: I do not know whether you have understood about our young people. We do not have the same attitude toward these matters as you do in the West."

Chia misjudged my opinion, however, for the fact is, everything I saw confirmed what she claimed—that the Chinese youth are not casual about sex or any form of personal relationship. Further, the energies and idealism of China's youth are constantly channeled into notions of service to society: and again, the youth are totally free of any exposure to sexy films, magazines and advertisements. There is a practical consideration, too: where can the deed be done? There are eight students to a room at college, one family to a room at home, there are no back seats of automobiles and practically no mobility.

As for abortion, another official told me: "There is no law against it but, generally speaking, it is not approved of. It is not good for the mother. They use a modern method: it is sucked out with some instrument... I am not sure. If a woman really wants one she can get it."

None of the young people that I questioned about abortion seemed to have given it any thought whatsoever. Those I asked were married or unmarried and all between the ages of twenty and thirty-five. The Chinese are blunt and pragmatic about matters of this nature: they attach no question of religious or other morality to something like birth control or

150

abortion, appraising them in eminently practical terms. I believe they were absolutely honest when they said they knew of no one who had had an abortion. The method the official referred to—removal of the fetus by air pressure—is not a Chinese invention. It has been used in Scandinavian countries for some time.

Peking's blessing was withheld from the birth-control movement for many years. Evidence of its wide promulgation seen during my visit to China indicates that those who have long advocated its introduction on a sweeping, national level have won out. I was told a score of times that "China's strength is her people." This is a basic plank of modern Chinese Communist society: it could well have been the fundamental reason why birth control was not encouraged earlier. The first public statements regarding a need for a birth-control campaign were made in September, 1954, but nothing was done publicly until March, 1957, when Madame Li Teh-chuan, Minister of Health, pulled the switch. A saturation campaign of lectures, exhibitions, posters, classes, followed. A little over a year later, it stopped as suddenly as it started. Contraceptives were still available but the heat was off: the exhibits were closed and the teachers talked about some other vital issue. Then, with much less fanfare a couple of years ago, the birth-control movement started up again, this time with Peking's plenary blessing. Now it appears to be an integral part of the lives of the young marrieds. Posters encourage smaller families, lecture groups still go into factories to advise young women, but the need to stimulate a sense of frantic urgency has apparently been eliminated by birth control's wide and ever-growing acceptance.

This might be as good a place as any to mention that the Chinese women were always fastidiously clean and personally attractive. The younger people particularly, men and women, take scrupulous care of their teeth and nails. The women were every bit as fresh and dainty as their Western contemporaries despite the fact that, except for soap, they lacked most of the aids, such as talcum powder, deodorants, body oils, which we have been led to believe are essential for our germless welfare. For their monthly hygienic needs, they use homemade pads of disposable, coarse white paper.

The return drive to Peking took about an hour. It was twilight when we arrived back at the Nationalities Hotel. On the fourth floor, the bellboys were gathered around the television set in the lounge off the lobby.

"One, two, three, four," said the voice on Peking's only channel. They repeated the numbers: it was their evening lesson in English.

Going down the maroon-carpeted hall to my bedroom, I ran into Yu and Li. Yu stopped, smiled and said something. Li repeated it:

"Mr. Yu would like to know if there is anything you wish to say to him."

I said no, everything was fine, and went to my room. I do not know what Yu meant then and I am not sure now. It is quite possible that he was merely enquiring after my health, or perhaps he felt I wanted more information about the day's tour. Or perhaps Peking had unearthed and passed on to him my true identity, or simply discovered my earlier visa application and were giving me a gracious "out," an opportunity to come clean on my own and admit that I lived in America and worked for Hearst.

Phil Howell, who owned a department store in a large Australian country town, occupied the room next to mine. Fatigued from the day, we decided to go up to the tenth-floor lobby for a drink. There was no bar there in the American sense, just a large, sparsely-furnished lounge, with a small glass counter and a shelf with a dozen or so bottles of unidentifiable alcohol. We ordered a whiskey and the laugh we had when it

152

arrived did us both good. It was very sweet, more like a cordial, and very weak; it cost about 7 cents. I longed to talk to someone about my position: Phil, a kindly, white-haired gentleman, came dangerously close to hearing the truth. But, sitting in the darkening room, looking out the window at the flat sprawl of Peking, I faced the fact I could not share that worry and responsibility with anyone.

I could not shake off Yu's words of the previous day: "We are grateful to you for being sincere and open-hearted." I reminded myself of the crude propaganda that I had seen, of the general tone of Peking's official pronouncements. I told myself I was in China to get a story, not to improve East-West relations, and that my motives were good even if my legal situation wasn't.

Yet, if I were discovered, what would they do? I had been told by businessmen that the Chinese were most honorable to deal with, but were capable of "abrupt" action if they felt slighted. It would be dishonest, however, to pretend that the legalities of the situation—and any fear of penalty—were the sole cause of my concern. Nor was it solely a persistent curiosity to find out just what they would do if I were to tell them. The fact was I liked and respected the Chinese around me enormously: I wanted to communicate with them. Yet, my situation made this impossible. I wanted, in fact, to be what Yu had already called me, "sincere and open-hearted." It went against my grain to be any other way.

I determined that as soon as I reached Hong Kong I would write him a full explanation. Because of the events that followed, I never did.

13

We flew down to Shanghai
in one of the smaller Russian Ilyusians. It carried about sixty
passengers and again the only crew members that I saw were
the attentive stewardesses who handed out sweets before we
left the ground, and packets of cigarettes as soon as we were
in the air. It was a turboprop flight of about 2½ hours from
Peking's round-towered airport—a nicely landscaped terminal
with a king-size pool decorated with fountains and surrounded
by gardens at its entrance—to Shanghai's modest terminal in
the western suburbs. As far as size is concerned, all of Peking
airport could be dropped into Kennedy Airport and nobody
would notice.

Finding myself seated next to Li Tieh-fei, I told him to
feel free to ask me any questions about life in Australia or the
United States.

He looked at me intently but was silent. Finally he said:
"Everyone calls you Lisa. What is that? The name in your
passport is Elizabeth."

I said Lisa was an abbreviation for Elizabeth—that my
family preferred it to Lizzie.

"Call me Lisa if you want to," I said, adding, as if to rectify an international imbalance, "I'll call you by yours. What's Tieh-fei mean, anyway?"

I had to bite my lip to stop from smiling, because despite his increasing pallor as the flight progressed, Li appeared to blush.

"Oh!" he said, and laughed outright. "I really don't know what my mother had in mind. It means . . . well, another time I'll tell you."

Another long silence. I liked Li Tieh-fei: as a matter of fact, I liked Yu Shang-ven, the party official, and Wang Lien-yi, the other interpreter, too. But Li's English was far superior to Wang's, and a delight to listen to because of its extraordinary clarity. After a while Li said:

"Naturally, there are things I would like to ask. But we wish to please our guests while they are in China, Lisa, and we are not always sure what pleases them and what upsets them. We must be very careful lest, unwittingly, we offend a Western woman."

I was beginning to feel like a little old lady. I suggested he stop worrying about it, and that our conversations proceed with a sense of trust and not fear, one of the other.

"That is true," said Li. "It is indeed a pity for people to come such a long way to visit another country and for those people not to be able to be sincere, not to be able to trust each other."

I turned and he was looking fully, but impersonally, at me. Deliberately, I changed the subject and asked about juvenile delinquency.

He replied, with discernible modesty and some hesitation as he sought for the right words:

"Do you mean a love child?"

"No, I didn't, but now that you mention it, yes."

"It happens less and less, now hardly at all. It would be

absurd to deny the fact that we have some but each year it is decreasing. I understand that delinquency is a great problem in the United States: we cannot understand this. Our young people all have something to do, there is no time left for such things.

"They study so many hours a day, and when school is out they carry on their own projects. All participate in some community project, even the primary school children, such as planting gardens or pulling weeds. From the start they are taught to contribute to the country's progress, to the community."

I had no reason to disbelieve him; throughout the trip I watched for signs of vandalism and the only thing I turned up were some initials cut into a bamboo in some gardens at Soochow.

We then had a brief discussion about our civil-rights movement. Li, who said he was interested in literature, praised John Howard Griffin's *Black Like Me* but had never heard of James Baldwin. I did not ask him why, but from what I saw of officially "approved" literature, both domestic and foreign, Baldwin's books would not be acceptable because of their tone of sexuality and violence. Use of these elements in literature is regarded as socially detrimental.

I was asked if I had ever been to Harlem and if it was true that there were places in New York where a Negro couldn't sit down or get a drink of water. Would President Johnson's voting rights bill really bring equality?

I explained as best I could and touched on some of the complications in trying to get people sufficiently motivated to break the cycle of ignorance and antisocial behavior from one generation to the next. I said motivation must be just as great a problem in dealing with some of the peasant farmers in China and Li conceded that this problem, even in the Communist system, could be a hard nut to crack.

Li then asked me what education I had had and I told him I had a degree in sociology.

"Isn't that unusual, for a woman in the Western upper classes to be interested in social problems?" he asked. I assured him that my graduating class was filled with men and women from both the upper classes and lower classes, and that my own particular interest was social pathology—or crime and delinquency.

"And your children," he asked, "do you let them watch a lot of violence on television?"

"No," I said, remembering that I must be careful to speak as an Australian. "The children are limited to watching a couple of children's shows on the weekend and that is all. We are very strict about television."

"You have lived in America," he said goodhumoredly. "What are these beatnik people? We Chinese think they are crazy!"

"The Chinese aren't necessarily alone in this," I said.

Later, on another occasion, when the whole group was sipping tea on a terrace and watching the sun go down, I got into a conversation with an older Chinese official. When the attention of the others was diverted he asked me:

"Is it really true . . . we have read that some Western women are wearing dresses that have no top to them?"

I laughed at this, a bit grimly perhaps, for it seems the Chinese image of Western morality is as far off base as the Western appreciation of Chinese morality.

"Just a few of them, a mere handful out of millions," I said.

He cautioned, trying hard not to look pleased at his own joke:

"Don't pretty yourself in Western style while here!"

It is obvious that although the Chinese have no illusions, or few, about the possibility of a Communist revolution in

America or Australia—"we know there is no seed of revolution there now, we know the workers are not really oppressed" I was told on one occasion—stereotype images of the middle and upper classes persist. It isn't hard to see why. The French, British, American, and other foreign residents who lived in their own "international" settlements in cities such as Shanghai, lived *la dolce vita* to the full: for the majority of these residents, but not all, the Chinese never came into consciousness as human beings and, if it weren't for the profit to be made from the Orient, it could have gone to hell in a handbasket. There is little that 2,000 foreign tourists a year—the record set in 1964—can do to eradicate or modify this image. Hopefully in time, with an expansion of tourist traffic, it will be modified more realistically.

Further, I had taken a prowl through the foreign language bookshop while in Peking and the only literature available in English were the novels of Elizabeth Gaskell, Sir Walter Scott, Thackeray, Dickens, and some short stories by H. H. Munro (Saki). Selections in the textbooks used by the English-major students at all universities included nothing more recent than some selections from George Eliot and some obscure, class-laden pieces by George Bernard Shaw. The workhouse scenes of Dickens appeared to be very popular.

I noticed at least two results of this literary boycott. One is that many of the translators speak a fluent and pure English that is frequently superior to that of the tourist. Secondly, many Chinese seem to be unaware of the vast changes in social consciousness that have taken place in the Western world in the past fifty years. Their view of the West socially, if not technically, is often strictly nineteenth century.

I spoke with so few Chinese that it would be madness to arrive at any generalizations, yet I was greatly struck by the ignorance of the extent and depth of the growth of social consciousness in the West displayed by the younger people with whom I did converse. This gap in their understanding of our own growing social sensitivity appeared to me to be colored by their own sense of a holy cause. It would be wrong to say that all Chinese with whom I spoke indicated they had a monopoly on justice and compassion but there was often more than a hint of moral superiority. This claim to moral superiority was often presented with such subtlety that an opportunity to challenge it was all but out of the question.

Here is a case in point. One night in Peking, the same night I told Yu that I had worked for the Hearst newspapers while living in the United States, we got into a discussion of world social conditions. I spoke about conditions in Mexico. I described the conditions there, including the vast and evident poverty both in the major cities and in the villages, where conditions are similar to those in the days of the Conquistadors.

When I finished Yu said:

"We are touched that you feel for the poor of these villages and that your heart goes out to the oppressed. It shows you are not indifferent to the lot of the poor and have some feelings for them, despite the fact that you are not one of them."

My hackles rose: of course I felt for the unfortunate! Almost as quick as this reaction was an understanding that Yu was a revolutionary and to this breed words are cheap. Action alone has value. What had I ever done that entitled me to claim credit for being "on the side" of the poor? I was left with no protest.

The plane now slid down through the thin clouds: below were little clusters of sepia-colored villages and checkerboard fields in green and brown. The hostess went through the plane gently waking the passengers and motioning for them to fasten their seat belts. Our interpreters pulled out their baggage from under the seats. (None of them carried more than a flight bag for the three-week tour; one felt that any sign of

159

surplus personal possessions, even if they owned them, was contrary to their almost monastic spirit—and besides, there was no need. Laundry and dry-cleaning facilities at Chinese hotels are excellent: a suit left out at night will be ready cleaned and pressed in the morning. After each hotel stopover, our officials appeared band-box fresh.) Li looked sick; on enquiry he said he had only a headache. I offered aspirin but he refused, saying it might make him sleepy. I said it wouldn't and he took them, perhaps to be polite, but later remarked: "Those things are good. They really work!"

I had the impression that the minor aches of everyday living don't merit much attention in today's China.

Two interpreters and a party official were at the Shanghai Airport to shake hands and smile us a welcome as we stepped off the plane onto the ramp. All the greeting and hand shaking made us feel like big shots and now we had six officials to our group of eleven. (China hopes to double its number of tourists in 1966 and I wondered at times if our group was providing practice runs for the herds to follow!)

The airport building at Shanghai is a modest affair compared to Peking, which has obviously been built in anticipation of a great increase in tourism. Shanghai Airport is extremely modern with a lot of glass, but box-like and small. We piled into our sparkling bus, the cleanliness of which we now took for granted, and drove into Shanghai.

What is it like, this former Las Vegas of the Orient? The agricultural areas around the airport gave no indication of its wild past. The streets were busy, not with motor traffic, but streams of women and children pushing and hauling carts of market produce. The women, as in the rural areas of Kwangtung Province, often hauled with a strap around their waist or shoulders, like draft animals. Again, I was surprised at how close China's agriculture is to her cities.

As we rode further into Shanghai, traces of the past began to assert themselves. Here, on broad, tree-lined streets, were

160

blocks of old mansions: so distinctive was the character of each of these homes that I played a game of guessing who formerly lived there.

There were gabled, Tudor-style homes, with sharp roofs originally designed to slough off snow; red-brick French provincial with dormer windows; stately, gray Italian villas with their once-formal gardens now overrun and the rococo fountain now at a tilt; weeds on the gravel driveway and purple hydrangeas trailing over the high, excluding walls.

Now the traces of old-time grandeur were more clearly delineated in the main arteries that swept down to the Bund, the internationally famous boulevard along the waterfront: they were broad, busy, filled with countless little boutiques, specialty bakeries, large department stores with bright and attractive window displays. On the Bund, we swung around to the Peace Hotel (which old China "hands" knew as the old Cathay Hotel owned by the British millionaire industrialist, Sir Victor Sassoon). The Huangpu (Whangpoo) River was cluttered with traffic, even in the heavy smog of late afternoon. There were countless freighters plying its yellow flow, two passenger vessels of perhaps 12,000 tons, and ferries bustling back and forth from the busy, thickly populated east side. The air was filled with ship sounds: shrieking, blasting, tooting. The noise drifted up to my room on the fourth floor.

Yet this, my first impression of a busy and cosmopolitan city, was to be greatly modified within a matter of hours and a closer look.

What was Shanghai like in former days? This is how an article by W. Robert Moore described it in *The National Geographic Magazine* of September, 1932:

"On the side streets are window displays worthy of any Fifth Avenue store; on cross-streets shops are hung with bright-colored flags, covered with Chinese ideographs, telling of bargains, sales, and the nature of the goods supplied.

"Modern talking cinemas, presenting the latest films, and

some high-class Chinese theaters debauch their gay night throngs.... Bright limousines unload a group of people at some large hotel along the Bund to attend a formal dinner; other people are frequenting wealthy Chinese restaurants. A mission is giving soup and religious teaching to a queue of hungry souls.... A woman beggar, carrying a poorly dressed babe, holds her hand out toward an ermine-wrapped lady who is carrying a Pekingese dog....

"Launches, lighters and sampans maneuver about.... Even women beggars comb the waters and hover around the ships to salvage in nets food scraps or anything else of use thrown overboard...."

It was a city where everyone hustled for their slice of life's pie, where prostitutes plied their trade and opium addicts supplied themselves by pimping. It was a city of shimmering nightclub life, bars that never closed, dance halls and dolls, of horse racing, gambling and glamour. Every morning bodies of unwanted babies were pulled out of the river, and if there was a sudden cold snap extra rubber-tired carts had to be hauled into service to take away the bodies of the rickshaw drivers found frozen stiff in the doorways.

Shanghai today is like a reformed madam: the physical proportions are still bounteous and there is a sense of old-time grandeur that cannot be erased. But with the same vitality that Shanghai once poured into libidinous pleasure she now pours into rigid purity. She will laugh and she will play—as long as it is within the limits prescribed by "plain living and high thinking." There is no gambling, no drinking, and prostitution has been erased as efficiently as the plague. There are few neon lights: at ten o'clock the radio station closes down, the *Tashihchieh*, the multi-amusement center, closes down, the streets empty, the city sleeps. Until that hour, one can go to a movie where thundering films about Viet Nam or the Japanese invasion are shown; to the opera, modern or classical, where the oppressions of the past are nightly acted out; or to the theater, where once again one is reminded that no matter who was on top before Liberation, the Chinese man-on-the-street was on the bottom. The luxury of the costuming, the color and arrangement of the often flamboyant choreography, the music—Chinese orchestras, whether playing with Western or traditional instruments, are first-rate—provide the only escape, if it is escape from the toils of hard work that is sought. And every theater was as jampacked as a New York subway car at rush hour.

A walk on the streets reveals that the shop-window decorations are excellent, although the goods available inside are recommendable mainly for their hard-wearing, utilitarian qualities. There are underwear, handkerchiefs, thick stockings, all "sensible," the sort of gear one takes to boarding school. Enamel dishes, once a luxury in China, are now purchasable everywhere; aluminum kettles hang from the smaller stores like lamps.

The bakeries in Shanghai were typical of those I saw in China. They greatly surprised me, for they were full of a variety of bread-like rolls, biscuits, dumplings and all sorts of pastry treats. And these stores were always crowded. They seemed to be one of the few businesses untouched by 100 per cent "plain living." Incidentally, there are also a lot of candy stores: the sweets and things such as ginger and walnuts treated in a number of ways. The caramels and such were all individually wrapped.

Past these store windows the residents of Shanghai stream on foot. The city has little road traffic. The Bund of Shanghai, one of the largest cities in Asia, could boast only light traffic during the noon hour. There are pedicabs, no rickshaws. On the outskirts of the city there is little empty land: factories, schools and tract houses stand on an area that my old, pre-Liberation map indicates as wasteland. Where the old Golf

Club once stood at the corner of Hungjao and Rubicon Roads is the new West End Park, complete with zoo. The People's Square now occupied the area once used for the race course. All the old, once privately owned department stores are still in business, but the names have been changed.

The former churches downtown are identifiable by their architecture, although the crosses are down on some but not all. Some are used as meeting halls or office buildings, others are still in use as Christian churches. In the outer suburbs the canals, once a source of pestilence, have been filled in; there are new roads, and a wanderer feels that indeed, "the old order changeth giving place to the new."

Yet, despite its former dog-eat-dog existence, there must have been a great deal of laughter in Shanghai. I regret that when Madame Shanghai reformed, she threw this precious baby out with the bath.

14

In each city we visited

we went to the theater, but it was in Shanghai that I witnessed the ultimate in adherence to Mao Tse-tung's statement that "there is no such thing as art that is detached from or independent of politics."

Theater in China today isn't a fringe benefit for the few: it occupies a role in the life of the ordinary city resident that television occupies in the United States, in the sense of being the chief hobby or diversion for after work hours. There the resemblance ends, for if theater in China has one single characteristic it is a total, uncompromising anger in remembrance of things past. It is indeed a vast catharsis, the greatest channel through which China today is expressing its anger, ventilating its humiliation, over its systematic decimation as a great nation over the years by internal corruption and external, foreign forces. To see Chinese theater is to strip away much of the confusion surrounding China's stance on the international scene: when a person—or a country—expresses without restraint his hurt, fury, humiliation, and hopes, his

165

actions, perhaps previously seeming bizarre, often begin to make sense. This was my reaction to Chinese theater.

It's a fact of revolution that art in any form is requisitioned as a component part of the revolutionary machine: in China, it has become the adrenalin in the national bloodstream. It draws on the nightmares of the past with inexhaustible fervor to point up the good of the present: with astonishing virility it distributes and keeps alive its bad memories. The visitor might be infuriated, filled with satiric glee, saddened or quietly maddened, but the very ferocity and authenticity of the passion expressed preclude one reaction— boredom.

There appeared to be little up-to-the-minute drama: it is necessary to go back at least fifteen years if the fires of past hell are to be kept stoked—American imperialism excluded. And this is the main function of Chinese theater today— uniting the people against the old enemies, dead or alive.

My initial acquaintance with Chinese theater in Canton has been mentioned, as has the anti-Johnson Administration play put on by the University of Peking students. However, compared to the force and vitality of China's most successful ballet, the *Red Army's Women's Detachment*, the students' message had the impact of a day-old cream puff.

The ballerina was China's finest and the show was televised. This would be for group viewing in places such as workers' recreation clubs, as there are no privately owned television sets; those I mentioned earlier in the communes were, of course, community property. As usual, there was an overflow audience of workers; they carried their soft cloth hats in their chipped and calloused hands. There were times when I thought that the audience, rather than the entertainment, might well be the ultimate achievement of Chinese theater. Theater of all kinds, including noisy and long classical opera, is enormously popular, so much so that there were times when I wondered if a certain number of attendances weren't somehow compulsory, or at least earned the worker good points. I asked young, serious-faced Wang if this was the case and he smiled slowly and said in his hesitating English:

"It is that the Chinese people have always loved theater." Yet I couldn't help but notice how happy he looked one night when the group, pleading fatigue, begged off after two hours of classical opera.

Every theater that I was in, or passed by and took a peek into, seemed to bear out his contention that theater in China occupies a high place in the people's lives. They were packed to the rafters, and not by people whose features or hands reflected a former upper-class background. By the worn appearance of their clothes, clean but patched, by their weather-beaten skin, their tough-skinned hands, they were obviously laborers and mechanical workers; their wives, dressed just as they do in the day in gray or navy without jewelry or make-up or any touch of frivolity, were often as not with them. The men congregated in the lobby at intervals, turning it into one cloud of smoke; the women remained in the theater.

The ballet, set on the island of Hainan, told the story of the girl Chuang Hua, vassal of a cruel landlord. In the opening scenes, she is whipped for an attempted escape. It is a scene of devastating, raw emotion: she struggles, writhing, her long black hair tumbling while the landlord, wearing a white, Western-style suit and sunglasses, supervises, at whim joining the whipping with a long, knotted rope. Ultimately, helped by courageous and sympathetic fellow servants, Chuang Hua flees and hides in the forest.

There, she meets two young men who listen with anger at her familiar story. Chuang Hua doesn't know it but they are members of the Communist underground. Chuang Hua hasn't even heard of the Communist party; they send her on to their camp.

At their secret hiding place, high in the mountains, Chuang Hua sees the red flag for the first time. As the audi-

167

ence wept, she embraced it. After training with other girls she goes into battle to capture the landlord's holdings. But she is "politically immature," the libretto says. When she sees the landlord, her own personal emotions overcome her. She fires at him prematurely in anger, forgetting the real meaning of "team work." As a result, the entire operation fails.

Shamed and ostracized, she returns to camp to do some political homework aimed at showing her that personal emotions are nothing; they must be set aside and overcome for higher goals. Finally, she battles the Kuomintang as the Communist male leader is burned to death. If my hair could stand on end it would have done so in the final scene, full of thundering sound and blazing color as all the women danced *en point* with rifles and fixed bayonets.

The audience was now on its feet and some of our interpreters were too moved to interpret. As the superb seventy-five-piece orchestra—playing a Chinese score reminiscent of Tchaikovsky—thundered to the finale, I looked at other Western guests. They looked stunned. No one was unmoved.

This was the first of two times that I was to see rosy-cheeked young girls dancing with fixed bayonets. Nor was there the slightest doubt as to the nature of the bayonet-fixed rifles within these dances: they were not dramatic decorations. They were weapons used with a dance step and arm position that lunged in short, horrible jabs and then thrust upwards.

It was a sobering, saddening sight, an almost intolerable contrast to the gentleness and warmth around me. Some of the group voted to walk back to the hotel, but I wanted none of it. I wanted the privacy of my hotel room, for I felt shaken to the verge of tears. Li sat next to me in the bus.

"You spent eight years in the army," I said, without doubt belligerently. "You know what bayonets are used for, their specific use, I mean."

He passed his hand across his eyes as if he were tired.

168

"Yes," he said.

"Well, do you like the sight of these girls dancing ballet with bayonets? Is it a pleasant sight? It doesn't look very peaceloving to me. What are you trying to do?"

Again he was silent and finally said, very quietly,

"I wonder, have you ever given any thought to whose fault it is that the girls of China are dancing with bayonets and not. . . ." he hesitated.

"Babies?" I suggested.

"All right," he said, "bayonets and not babies in their arms?"

Maybe I should have argued but there was little fight left in me that night. I felt as if I'd been run over by a truck.

Yet, the following day, there was to be more of the same. That might make it sound as if the trip was becoming untenable—in fact, it wasn't getting any easier. We were well and courteously cared for: if we wanted something special every attempt was made to arrange for it. But what I was finding increasingly hard to take was the unremitting exposure to the ferocious, almost primeval, energy and force of Chinese theater today. It was in the Children's Cultural Palace that I witnessed the ultimate in Chairman Mao Tse-tung's teachings regarding art and politics.

The "palace," an old rambling house with little grates for coal fires, was formerly one of Shanghai's old mansions. Now it is an after-school center for children from the crowded downtown area. It provides a variety of learning-through-play experiences, with electrical toys and gadgets, as well as offering music and choral lessons.

The lines of smiling, clapping children attested to our expected arrival: a little bright-eyed boy or girl took our hands firmly and smiled at us with shy approval as we were led through the freshly scrubbed building. In one room, a group of boys were all but oblivious to our presence as they labored on their model airplanes. In other rooms, there were accordion and mouth organ classes. In another, there were twenty-eight children taking down Morse code at the rate of fifty words a minute. They were aged about ten.

Our little guides, dressed in corduroy slacks and pretty, bright sweaters, were filled with a justifiable pride at their "palace." Chinese children are extremely well-mannered and these were exceptional in their poise. They led us into one room where a group of little girls about seven years of age, dressed in the costumes of the minority nationalities, danced for us, May-poling around a large picture of Mao Tse-tung, singing:

> I think of you in the morning
> And I think of you in the night
> And when I awake I am smiling.

Then some lively little boys made their contribution with this song:

> I get up in the morning
> My father is holding the gun
> And my mother is going to the parade
> And we are shouting at the parade:
> "Support the Viet Namese people against American imperialism."

In the attic the finale awaited us—a play by six children, aged seven to ten entitled, *Five Letters About Viet Nam*. Two tourists left to wait outside: the woman director indicated no whit of awareness that tourists might be affronted at seeing children so politically embroiled.

A little girl, in red dirndl skirt and white blouse, her hair pulled to a curl on each shoulder, said she had just received five letters about Viet Nam. As she spoke her voice started to build up and then, one by one, each child came in from the

170

wings to say his or her piece. Japan, Indonesia, Africa, and South Viet Nam were represented. The little boy representing Africa had his face coal-blackened.

The depth of the passion these children expressed as they urged the "U.S. aggressors to get out of Viet Nam" was unattractive to witness. Were they superbly trained actors, was it a game, or did they know precisely what they were acting out?

Then they broke up and clasped our hands and as we left they all called out, smiling:

"Come back, Uncles and Aunties, come back."

That night I went to the Great World, the multi-amusement center off Nanking Road. This city-block long, four-storied building was the hangout for prostitutes and drug addicts before Liberation: old China hands remember it as a good place in which to get mugged. Now it is a cultural and amusement mecca. It is open seven nights a week from 7 to 10 p.m. and a dime will admit anyone to any of the ten plays, operas or variety shows, all of which are running simultaneously. For a light touch, there are fun-house distorted mirrors downstairs (I stood reflected in one with a little old Chinese gentleman with a spidery beard and we shrieked at the way we looked together!) and upstairs there's a shooting gallery and a few pinball machines. I noticed this area was practically deserted while again, at the serious operas and plays, the audience was standing at the back six deep. So totally intent on the play was one group, that we finally gave up trying to break through the crowd to reach our seats in front. Those too far back to hear, or those hard of hearing, are helped in understanding the play or opera by the use of lantern slides which flash the story and the dialogue to the side of the stage, as it unfolds.

I picked up the rifle on the shooting range and hit a moving duck. Ho, the local Shanghai interpreter, said: "Good shot!" I shot again and got another bull's-eye. Ho said: "You shoot remarkably well." I shot again, again on dead center. This time Ho asked me where I learned to shoot and I told him: rabbits in Australia.

In one room at the center was one of the many exhibitions I saw in China designed to do away with superstition and encourage scientific understanding. This was without doubt the best exhibition of this kind that I saw. These displays are primarily designed to catch those citizens who are either too young or too old to attend school, or for some reason are on the fringe of academic programs.

This exhibition included two fetuses in different stages of development, and a fully developed baby, all in bottles, a bit shocking to some foreigners perhaps but apparently not the least upsetting to the browsing Chinese. Signs in the display pointed out that feudal rulers kept the Chinese under oppression by fear and superstition.

One poster read:

"There are no such things as ghosts. Birthmarks are not caused by ghosts. Ghosts do not pull out the hair and cause baldness."

There were models of the human body; a display showing how rain is formed and how man is beginning to predict and to some extent control the weather; and also a display refuting geomancy (divination by means of lines or figures). As in all other similar displays, there was also a series of charts and illustrations on hygiene and disease.

I wanted to go to the opera but there were no seats available. We settled instead for the acrobatics and juggling, for which Chinese theater has long been famous. That night the acts seemed particularly skillful and amusing; I laughed until the tears came. But I could still hear the little children shouting about Viet Nam and, in the last analysis, it would be difficult to say whether I was laughing or crying.

15

This was to be our last day

in Shanghai and it was to prove a real workout. It started with
an interview with Chu Jue, the short, dapper, chain-smoking
director of the Bureau of Education in Shanghai.

Mr. Chu kindly came to the hotel, where Myra Roper and
I interviewed him in the sitting room of a most comfortable
suite.

I asked him what the aim of education was in China
today.

"The final aim is to eliminate any distinction between the
mechanical worker and the mental worker. All education
must serve proletariat politics. Our aim is to form cultivated
workers with a socialist consciousness."

"The principle used to achieve this aim is theory combined with practice: the contents of the text book must be
combined with productive labor," said Chu, whose words
were as neat and clear-cut as his appearance.

The first step in producing "the successors of the proletariat" is taken in primary school, where the pupil is encouraged
to perform deeds for the welfare of society, "such as cleaning
parks and streets."

"Children at full-time middle school (aged twelve to eighteen) spend one month a year at labor. This is often during the harvest season. When the students go to the countryside, the principal and teachers go and work with them."

Flicking his cigarette, Chu spoke decisively about those who would mollycoddle students.

"Those who worry about labor hampering students have a mistaken idea that schools should be cultivating intellectuals and not workers," he said.

"Those who don't go to communes to eat and labor with the peasants for a month, go into factories.

"They are prepared to go anywhere, into the mountains or into the country, for socialist construction."

Attendance at school, said Chu, is neither free nor compulsory, but there is 100 per cent attendance among primary school-age children in the city of Shanghai, 85 per cent attendance in the adjoining rural areas.

Primary school costs 6 yuan ($3) a semester and middle school (junior and regular high school) 12 yuan ($6) a semester. Semesters run from September to January, and from the end of February to the middle of July. Stipends are available for hardship cases in primary and middle schools— "Hardships such as the death or prolonged illness of one or both parents," said Chu.

All universities and institutes of higher learning are free, as is all medical care. Meals cost a few yuan, but again, these could be provided free "where need exists."

Chu said that there are 143,000 children in 1,400 kindergartens in the city: there is increasing emphasis on preschool education. There are 5,300 primary schools with a total attendance of 838,900 students. Of these students, 499,000 go on to middle schools, 50,000 of them eventually entering one of the city's twenty universities or higher institutes of learning.

This raises the question of what happens to the 339,000 primary school boys and girls who do not, for one reason or another, go on to middle school.

"Some 32,000 of them are attending experimental part-work, part-study schools," said Chu. "They are built either adjacent to a factory for technical students or on the communes for agricultural students."

Chu said some of the students were at specialized agricultural colleges, others were in part-study, part-farm labor institutes. Those in the colleges would become agricultural scientists. Even so, adding up the statistics Chu gave me—7,000 in technical schools, 20,000 at farm-work study schools, 15,000 at agricultural colleges, 32,000 at technical part-work, part-study schools, for a total of 74,000—it is apparent that of the city's 838,900 students at primary school nearly one-third get no academic training after the age of twelve.

However, the most meaningful measurement of China's achievement in its efforts to educate its masses can't be obtained by comparing present standards with other countries, but rather the distance Chinese education has traveled in the past fifteen years. Not for one minute do the Chinese conceive of having "arrived": they constantly reiterated the fact that their journey has barely begun. If there is anything like 100 per cent primary school attendance in Shanghai, even if it does end for one-third of all children at the age of twelve, it is infinitely better than anything the city has ever achieved in education before. Prior to 1950, only one child in every three got any schooling whatsoever.

Just as apparent as their accomplishments is the admitted fact that thousands of city teenagers are being separated from their parents and sent by school authorities to the country, there to put down rural roots and work the land. When I asked Chu if the children and parents had any choice, he replied crisply:

175

"The personal will of our students must meet the needs of our country," which is another way of saying they have no choice.

I persisted in my question: what if one of the parents was ill and the child needed at home? Chu said that exceptions could be made, but, "generally speaking, the parents are happy their children are working for socialist construction."

The love, gentleness and respect between Chinese children and their parents are wonderful things to see. It was also my observation that the Chinese are behind their government's efforts at socialist construction: but when Chu claimed that parents were happy to let their children go, I felt he was totally mistaken.

Chu was now speaking about the shortage of teachers that had followed the "great leap forward" in education. One result of the desperate shortage is that primary teachers—who require only graduation from middle school to qualify—are now middle school teachers. Normally, middle school teachers require two years at "normal" university (roughly equivalent to junior college).

Teachers earn about 75 yuan ($37.50) a month.

Chu said an attempt is being made to raise teaching standards by setting up Pedagogue Institutes in every district to continue their education and give further academic assistance to both "teachers and principals."

The curriculum is the same for all students: political science; culture, such as study of the Chinese language; physics, mathematics and "labor."

Asked for a definition of the political science course, Chu said:

"The content is solely the study of Marxism-Leninism and the thinking of Chairman Mao Tse-tung which governs Communist morality."

There are 370,000 adults in Shanghai's night schools and they take only political science and culture.

"This culture consists of writing poems, singing, perhaps staging a musical festival such as a recent one, *The Spring of Shanghai*. Housewives who were illiterate before, now read the newspapers. There are only a few older persons, mainly old women, who are still illiterate in Shanghai today."

Chu said that four intensive illiteracy drives have been conducted since 1950. The last ended in 1964, for which Chu claimed 99 per cent success.

The high rate of night school attendance can be explained simply because higher skills receive higher wages. Further, there is unremitting pressure to upgrade oneself both in mental and physical skills. One interesting example of this is Shanghai's Workers' Spare-Time University which caters to "creative and inventive workers." Chu said that it had produced over 2,000 technical innovations for the workers to take back to their factories.

At the conclusion of the interview, Chu summed it up patly:

"The workers are now the masters of this country."

From the hotel, we went by cab to the Shanghai Machine Building School to look at one of the part-work, part-study institutes in action. Mrs. Chiang, a local translator who had interpreted for Chu, came with us. She was an exceptionally neat, cool, and competent woman of about forty-five who, on our bus drives through the city, never failed to point out with unremitting firmness sites of former "imperialistic abuses." This included shops allegedly put out of business by the "dumping" of surplus goods by Americans; the former race course, now the People's Square, but once "a gambling hell established by imperialists"; and Huangpu Park, which once bore the infamous notice "Dogs and Chinese not allowed." It wasn't as blunt as that but that was the gist of the message. Someone remarked that this notice was removed years before the Communist party took over Shanghai but Mrs. Chiang brushed off that suggestion with a short laugh.

177

The principal of the part-work, part-study institute was standing waiting outside the administration building with some members of her staff when we arrived. We were taken into an upstairs room where we were seated at a long table for tea and talk. On the wall above us were the usual pictures of Marx, Lenin, Stalin, and Mao. I had learned by now that during the introduction, which in this case was brief but which sometimes lasted up to half an hour, interruptions or questions of any sort were not welcome. At especially arranged interviews such as this, there was often a person, to whom we were not introduced, taking notes of the entire discussion. There was such a secretary at this interview.

The principal, Mme. Xu Nian Chu, said that there were 1,360 students aged sixteen to twenty in the school. There were 369 teachers. This remarkably high teacher-student ratio was typical of other schools I visited. Obviously, in view of the admitted teacher shortage, a choice had been made to teach less but teach well, rather than dilute the teaching—as well as the personal influence of the teacher—with classes of larger sizes. The choice seemed to me indicative of China's determination, not only to do what it does well, but above all else to consolidate the revolution.

The school was a resident college and those wishing to enroll had to compete with others in a city-wide examination. There are two semesters in the year, between which the students go home to see their parents. Not all go at the same time, however, as vacations are staggered. The reason for this is that the factory on the school grounds is in all-year-round production making lathes, jacks and thermostats.

A total of ninety weeks' labor in the factory is a prerequisite for graduation, so the students spend one week in their classroom and then one week in the factory. Of these ninety weeks, seventeen must be in the student's speciality.

The curriculum calls for six class hours a day from 8

a.m. to 2 p.m. All periods are fifty minutes long. There are four periods a week each on "political science" and mechanical drafting; both these subjects are compulsory. In addition, they must take mathematics and physics, and either Russian or English.

Asked if they studied Chinese history, Mme. Xu said no, that they had completed this subject in middle school. They study no history of any other country. The students have Saturday afternoon and Sunday free for political lectures and discussions, or for straight free time. Sometimes they attend the movies across the street.

Medical and dental work is available free on the school grounds, Mme. Xu said. All the students do their own washing and cleaning but meals are provided in a communal dining hall.

All teachers at this school spend two days a week at labor in the factory. Often the teams into which they are put are led by students whose manual skills are more advanced.

When they graduate, students are certified as Technical Workers Grade II or III on the national scale which goes up to VIII. I asked if they then had the free choice of a job.

Mme. Xu answered by saying that "the needs of the country are first, and generally they go where the state tells them.

"Our aim is to cultivate students with a socialistic consciousness," said Mme. Xu, using words identical to those used earlier that morning by Chu Jue. "We aim for a medium level in culture plus some specific skill. We wish to cultivate the viewpoint of labor to strengthen ties with the working class. Take the production of thermostats. If that is a student's speciality, he must be able to start with a pencil and paper and a knowledge of the principles involved, design it and make it with his own hands."

This contrasted sharply with the increasing specialization of education in Western countries, and was, I thought, one of the most significant aspects of education in China, for a man who has been instilled with how each specific technological task fits into the basic principles of science is not dependent upon technology to maintain an industrial society. This man can build his own technology. On the other hand, the highly technically trained society that lacks an understanding of the basic principles of science has nothing on which to rebuild its technology if it is lost through some form of social catastrophe, and it must inevitably return to the jungle. For instance, insulin prolongs the lives of tens of thousands of people and is a household word for tens of millions, but because of the general ignorance of biochemistry's basic scientific principles, this product is a complete mystery except to a very few. Should these very few perish, the lack of knowledge of the basic principles involved by the vast majority of people would mean the whole process of tedious research to "discover" this life-giving serum would have to be started again. And so on in a thousand different ways.

Mme. Xu said that the students also made many of the machines and tools required for use in the factories.

As for "political science":

"It consists of studying the works of Chairman Mao Tse-tung, particularly his essays, *On Practice* and *On Contradiction*. No student can graduate until these principles have been mastered creatively."

I asked Mme. Xu what she meant by "creatively," and she said that the principles must be grasped in such a way that they could be used as practical mental tools to precipitate technical innovations and social progress.

We then toured the classrooms with Mme. Xu and her assistant, a man named Hu Wen Kuang. Mme. Xu told us she had had only one year of middle school. The civil war had intruded and she had later joined the Liberation Army. In other words, she had gone to school until she was thirteen.

Hu, on the other hand, was a graduate in aeronautical engineering from the University of Nanking. It was evident in all institutions I visited that proven political fealty to the regime took precedence over intellectual and academic qualifications.

The classrooms for beginners started off with a maximum of forty students, but by the time they reached their third and fourth year studies, there were only eight or ten students to a class. In one physics laboratory there were large framed pictures of Faraday and Newton. All the laboratory equipment, and the machines for testing metal resistance and stress, were made in China. The simple electrical equipment was all made by the students themselves.

In the classrooms, there was an atmosphere of informality but quiet purpose. There was no restriction on talking or movement: students moved freely and helped each other, but with barely any noise. The teacher seemed to have no special rostrum or place: he went from one group to another, helpful but not intruding.

In the factory there was the same contented atmosphere. White-capped, black-braided girls and young men worked side by side with their teachers in calm efficiency. Outside, a group of teen-age boys played basketball on the court; some girls, in navy slacks not unlike jeans and bright floral-print blouses, rinsed out clothes under the cold water of a trough. On the other side of the building, a group of teen-age boys were washing out their socks and laying them out to dry across a short bamboo pole that stuck from each dormitory window.

The school appeared to have been a school for many, many years. There was a massive dormitory building, play courts, a scattering of other red-brick buildings, including what had apparently been stables, all joined together by shady, tree-lined avenues. We had consumed hours of Mme. Xu's time but the manners of the Chinese are exemplary. Not once did I ever see any busy person glance at his watch—or give any

181

indication of impatience. We were conducted back to the car (an old black French Peugeot) with the same time-consuming formality with which we were received.

I was most impressed by this institute: in its plainness and utilitarian style it reminded me of a convent boarding school I attended as a teenager. The contentment of the students, living a community life with their teachers in a round of study, chores, and play, was plainly visible. They were totally free of the time-consuming, mind-consuming burden of being attractive and "in." The very simplicity of their clothes and demeanor, the orderliness of their lives, their air of dedication and purpose, made a devastating contrast to educators' reports of some of the problems in our own high schools.

This school, of course, was one of the best institutes. It wasn't on the regular tourist's schedule, but undoubtedly it was one of those to whom tourists were sent if they requested a visit to this type of institution. It was the air of whole-hearted dedication that struck me at this institute, but it was in no way different from the spirit I perceived at the three other educational institutions that I visited.

From the school we returned to the hotel, and joined the rest of the group going to another project that proved to be every bit as interesting as the part-study, part-work experiment. This was the Thao Ying Workers' Settlement in the Huangpu district.

This settlement is essentially a modern attempt at decentralization of the downtown area. It comprises 11,000 families, or a total of 60,000 persons, rehoused in a planned community, with complete shopping facilities, in the Shanghai outer suburbs. These families lived in conditions almost identical with those described earlier in the housing projects adjoining the textile mill in Peking, with light, gas, running water, shared kitchen, and toilet.

We were briefed by the head of the Street Committee, a

well-built, fine looking man named Han, whose manner was at once direct and warm. He was one of the most outgoing officials I met in China: I noticed as he crossed the yard that children crowded around him as if he were the pied piper. He had a smile for them all.

This settlement included not only six primary and six middle schools, but also a complete shopping center, a park of several acres with a large lake, a cultural "palace," and a hospital. Three bus lines ran directly to the city from the settlement night and day.

The average wage of the residents was 80 yuan ($40) a month, and rent was 5 per cent of income. All the working residents were employed in factories adjacent to the settlement. Included on the grounds was a small orphanage so that any children who were left bereft would not have to be removed from familiar surroundings and long-time family friends. Han said that occasionally a child would lose one or both parents through illness or death because of the poor conditions prevalent in China when their parents themselves were children. One had no way of knowing how many "occasionally" was meant to indicate.

There were happy, well-fed, neatly dressed youngsters all over the place. The boys played football and basketball, the girls hopscotch. The director tried for a basket as we passed a court: when he made it, the kids loved it and so did he.

The dimensions and concept of this settlement were vast. There was nothing fancy anywhere, but all the buildings were solidly constructed, mainly of concrete blocks, and there was no sense of crimping or crowding. The apartment buildings were two-storied but were designed to take more floors: some had already been added to.

We stopped at one apartment, a single room, with some fifty books in a bookshelf, embroidered pillow slips, floral curtains and everything spick and span.

The owner, a tall woman with short, permanently-waved hair, apologized, as women do everywhere, for the "confusion," adding that she had just returned from her annual vacation in Hangchow. She was a teacher of Chinese in a spare time school and her husband worked across the street in the power plant. All her education, she said, had been gained after her twenty-fifth year: she had come from a peasant family and war and poverty had precluded any schooling.

I asked Li what the conditions of these people had been before, and he replied:

"Lisa, I don't think you can imagine!"

Before leaving, I thanked Han and congratulated him on the project. In passing I referred to India and said how desperately such projects were needed there. It was interesting to note—for this was the second time I had received a similar reply when India was mentioned—that Han said most stiffly and formally:

"I know nothing of that! It is up to each country to solve its own problems."

The last stop of the day was at the Workers' Cultural Palace, a downtown recreation center. Formerly Shanghai's Grand Hotel, its activities are financed by a contribution of 1 per cent of salary by workers to their unions. What an extraordinary sight! From lobby to top floor, every room had something different going on.

In the old grand dining room there were a bunch of twenty-year-old boys as lively as a barrel of chimps doing acrobatic workouts, which that evening included getting ten of themselves onto an ordinary, two-wheel bicycle! In another room, two girls and a man sat yowling, and occasionally giggling, as they tried out their separate roles in traditional Chinese opera. Downstairs, the older men played billiards, while others read in the library awaiting their turn at the table.

184

There were a score of different groups of young girls, some from the same factories, others brought together by a liking for song or dance.

The songs were what we had by now come to expect: *Chairman Mao Is a Member of Our Commune*, *We Shall Follow Chairman Mao Forever*, and *Get the U.S. Imperialists out of Viet Nam*. Then, to everyone's astonishment, the same group burst into *Clip, Clip, Go the Shears*, a folk song, very old, from the outback of Australia—sung in Chinese! Had I told them that I was from the United States, they probably would have burst into a Chinese version of *We Shall Overcome*. The energy spent for, and honoring, their guests seemed to be limitless.

By far the best, however, was kept until the last—full orchestras playing westernized Chinese music with traditional Chinese wood and wind instruments. There is a strain of incredible melancholy in this music: much of what was played for us that night were songs from the outlying tribes of the far-west minority groups. On enquiry I was told the government had undertaken a long-term project to preserve, by actually writing down the notes of sounds, the words of songs, and making recordings of the traditional, perhaps ancient, music of these far, lonely provinces.

I was so grateful to have heard this music! It was communication and I was hungry for it. With its delicate strain and haunting melody, it could not have been further removed from the children's Vietnamese theatrics of the day before. It seemed to push China back into historical focus.

16

About 500 B.C.,
the time of Confucius, Socrates, Pericles and Buddha, the city of Soochow was built. Laid out in what was then the jungle and swamp of the Yangtze River delta, it was famous for its system of irrigation and drainage canals a thousand years before Venice existed.

Now our train was rushing toward it. Yu, sitting opposite me, fished a piece of string from his tunic pocket and showed me how to make cat's cradle, a popular game with Chinese children. He showed me a couple of little tricks and beamed when I couldn't catch on. His energy and good humor were boundless: he would have been a rare individual anywhere for he seemed to enjoy every moment to the hilt. He was also a great talker—when it came to discussing Communist doctrine: it was like springing a trap. The dialectics poured out of him and it was not hard, just impossible, to get a word in edgeways. He would wave his hands, raise his voice a little, grin a little apologetically for his enthusiasm but not slow down one whit. The only way to get a word in was to outshout him. It was all done in good humor. He showed lit-

186

tle curiosity about the Western world: I felt that whatever we said was accepted with a grain of salt. For instance, on one train trip I made a real attempt to try to convey to him some of the social, human problems that emerge in a technically advanced and affluent society. I embarked on this project because I had grown a bit weary of the constant suggestion that one politico-economic system holds the key to all the ills of all countries of the world. When I touched on employment, he said:

"There is much unemployment in the United States."

"There is some," I said, "and it will grow worse as automation and cybernation take over."

Li hesitated for a moment over "cybernation."

"Call it the black-box revolution," I suggested. Heavens knows how the translation sounded in Chinese. Anyway, Yu replied:

"It is unusual for someone to admit to unemployment in the United States."

"Really?" I said. "The figures are published all the time in American newspapers. Unemployment in America runs pretty constant at 4 per cent of the population."

"I have seen pictures of workers demonstrating for jobs," said Yu, "hundreds of them in the street."

I said that this was not so: as I denied it, Yu smiled politely. I felt he didn't believe me; at the same instant, I wondered if pictures of civil-rights demonstrations had been passed off in China as unemployment demonstrations.

Trips like this one to Soochow never lost their sense of excitement for me; yet now my excitement was overshadowed by the knowledge that the tour would soon be over and in a few days I would be outside China, perhaps barred from reentry for good. Once that happened, there would never again be a chance to explain, face to face, to these Chinese what I had done and why I did it. Yu, for instance, would learn sec-

187

ondhand of my deception: he and Li wouldn't be human if they would not regret bitterly the open-hearted kindness that they daily extended to me. In fact, all that I had said regarding the United States, civil rights, employment, would become suspect.

I took a long look at Yu as he labored over a particularly tricky cat's cradle. About forty-three years old, he was about 5 feet 10 inches tall, olive-skinned, with fine, dark brown wavy hair. He had large, white protruding teeth that lent his face a perpetual expression of good humor, as if he were always on the verge of laughter, which was indeed the case! Like most Chinese, there didn't appear to be an iota of fat on his long, gangling body; his hands were typically Chinese: slim, long-fingered, incredibly dexterous.

"Yu," I asked through Li, "tell me about yourself."

He chuckled at that: he was a very humble, ordinary person, but he would like to tell his story if I would like to hear. This is it as best as I can remember, a tale told to the whistle and the rocking of the train, to the flashing by of green fields. It was typical of stories that have been told and recorded scores of times by journalists and writers visiting China over the past thirty years.

"My father was a peasant farmer and we were very poor, but just like everyone else. My father worked for a landlord. There were about 200 families who rented land from him. Some of the landlords were just to their tenants, but ours was typical: we gave back 50 per cent of all the crops and on top of that had to pay taxes.

"We lived in a room, my sister, my brother and myself. My father worked all the time: he was gone in the dark and came back in the dark but there was not enough, never enough food and we were cold in winter. When I was six I went to work for the landlord looking after his cows. That was my job, to make sure they didn't wander. Sometimes they did,

188

or sometimes he was angry: he would beat me across the back if I came near him. It would be very cold in the morning.

"My mother talked to my father about my going to school, and always we hoped from year to year that maybe I could learn to read and write, because then my father would know when he was being cheated on the harvest and the taxes. When I was nine I went to school for the winter months and learned some figures.

"Every spring festival the peasants had a little celebration and they would eat a dumpling with their rice. I had always heard about the dumpling in the rice and each year my mother said, 'Be patient, one day we will have a dumpling in our rice.'

"But we never had enough surplus to get the dumpling. My mother tried: that's a woman's pride, but things always seemed to be getting worse.

"On the eve of the spring festivals; that's when the landlord would send his men out to gather in the taxes. Often my father would have to flee and hide, because we didn't have any taxes to pay them: in a few days my father would come back again. My mother had a baby, a son, but it cried a lot and then it died: my mother had no milk in her breasts. Can you imagine? It died, my brother died, because we had nothing to give it.

"Then we heard the Communists were coming and we fled, the 200 families. We went to the mountains and another landlord there rented us land and it started all over again. A lot of the people died on the way: we ate grass and roots and the children died first, and then the old people.

"Then again we heard the Communists were coming. We knew how soldiers were: the Kuomintang had been through our homes and villages; we had to hide what we could because they took everything. They told us the Communists would kill us, burn our homes, and take our cattle.

"We huddled in the mountains for days after the Com-

189

munist army reached our village, but then we were hungry and some crept back in. Then we started hearing strange things—that the Communists weren't sleeping in our homes, but in the fields, and they were asking people for water and food but taking nothing unless it was offered. All our cattle were gone but the Kuomintang had driven them away before them, and now the Communists had sent out troops to get them back.

"When we saw the cattle coming back to the village we started coming down from the mountains ourselves; we put our chickens out to feed as the soldiers didn't steal them. It wasn't the way we had thought it would be. I remember how frightened I felt when I first saw a Communist soldier as I walked down the village street. Then they started teaching us that they were good and would help us get the land for ourselves. When I was a teenager I joined the Communist army and spent eight years in it. I was wounded twice. There is not much I can say about my old life. It was very simple and just like everybody else's. I am sorry about my brother: I have not forgotten him nor why he died. I do not wish such things to ever happen in China again."

Had Yu been tutored in advance with this story? After all, he was a party official and it would be normal to anticipate a tourist requesting his life story. Yu claimed this was his life story; if it wasn't, if the story was false, then Yu's life as a peasant farmer must have been an exception, for all the information I have been able to gather written by people in China prior to the Communist takeover indicates that conditions were, if anything, worse than those described by Yu.

We were somewhat subdued for the rest of the trip. I got up after a while and walked from the soft seat section down to the hard seats. I wandered through many carriages just mingling with the people. A couple of young women were breast-feeding their babies: there was plenty of milk, it spilled

190

over the babies' mouths. I thought that here, again, was an indication that the people were getting sufficient nourishment: furthermore, I didn't see any women breast-feeding babies any older than a year or so. In countries where adequate food for the children is lacking, women often resort to breast-feeding until the child is three or even four. Some of the men were playing cards. I felt a tap on my shoulder. It was Li. I felt a little angry.

"Look," I said quietly, "I'm safe and sound and I'm not bothering anyone. I'm tired of being excluded from ordinary people: I like it down here."

"Hush, you must consider, perhaps your presence here is making it difficult for these people, Lisa," said Li very softly. "Please, return to your carriage."

Now I was angry: it seemed at that moment that we were welcomed by the Chinese people only if we stayed within the narrow confines prescribed for us. Certainly, we were free to wander in the streets of the cities, through the villages, to mingle for moments with people who passed, but what chance was there, as there is on a trip to Italy or Sweden, to sit in companionable quiet with a simple family group and try, with facial expressions, gesture and laughter, to communicate? There was none! I started to try and explain, whispering, but now everyone was indeed staring at us.

"Come," said Li, jerking his head toward the section where the carriages joined. We stood there while the train swayed and jerked and looked at each other in despair.

"What is it? What's the matter?"

How could I define it? I scarcely knew myself what was the matter. It was like Kafka, people talking at one another, never to one another, all the words sensible but nothing quite making sense. There were moments, such as during Yu's story, when the whole group held its breath and understood the common language of humanity: but then a simple thing

191

like going to another carriage occurred and you were back in no man's land.

"There's so little freedom," I burst out.

Li lit a cigarette and looked at me intently.

"People think we have no freedom but such is not the case. What did the people have before, freedom to starve to death? You cannot understand—or can you?—that if you lived here, Lisa, how hard you would try to help the system, how much of yourself you would want to give to make sure things like that"—he jerked his head back toward Yu's direction—"never come to our people again. If you had seen it before, you would not hesitate to say, as all our young people say, 'I will do whatever the state wants.'"

But what of one's own, unique personal being, I protested; what of individual hope and desire—have they no value?

"There is no division here between the state and the good of the people. The state here works only for the people. We have many freedoms here of which you seem to be unaware."

I said, not caring if my words sounded like a taunt:

"You weren't even asked if you wanted this job!"

"I suppose this is the sort of thing you are told abroad," he said, with a slight trace of contempt. "Would you believe me if I told you I had a choice of jobs, four or five if I remember. This job was not my first choice, but the state needed interpreters and I was happy, can you understand that, happy to surrender my own personal will and do as the state wished. In this there is great freedom, Lisa: do you follow me?"

I said, yes, I understood the freedom that came with total, unquestioning surrender to a higher authority, or to a belief or faith, but that I viewed this type of surrender as extremely dangerous.

"In your country or in ours?" asked Li.

"What difference does that make?"

192

"Because our government does not make mistakes," he said simply.

The train had taken us perhaps thirty miles but Li and I were essentially right back where we started.

We spent two days in the tree-lined city of Soochow: there are thirty miles of canals within the city itself. It is surrounded by a wide and beautiful moat, connecting through water gates with an inner moat. This in turn connects with the canals. Girdling the moat are the remnants of the wall built 2,500 years ago: the present wall, ancient itself, rests on the original foundations. The streets run parallel to the canals, the gray stone homes facing the streets, the back door skirting the canals. Outside the door of each home, facing the street, was a well, no wider than a foot, through which the women drew pure water.

Soochow is a city where every stone has a story, every garden a tale. It is a city of names as extravagant or as delicate as the stories that are told—the Lion Garden, the Falling Rain Pavilion, the Pavilion of Far-Off Fragrance, the Hall of Fragrant Snow and Misty Cloud, Tiger Hill, and Precious Girdle Bridge.

No emperor or powerful prince founded this charming city: in fact, it was founded 500 years before Christ by what the history books call a barbarian. This barbarian was Ho Lu, whose strength became such that the princes of China united to toss him out into "the Great Beyond," the swampy, trackless wilderness of the Yangtze River delta. Here, Ho gathered his men around him, prospected the ground, tasted the water, observed the heavens, and planned the earth! They drained the swamps, cut the canals, and turned the valley into the granary of China. When Ho decided to build a capital city worthy of a king and his court, he picked the site of Soochow. A wall of defense, twenty-three miles in circumference, was

193

built. None of it remains today but there are large sections of the heavy, ten-mile-round inner wall standing virtually as they were built in 500 B.C. Centuries later, the canal system was joined to the Grand Canal, which runs from Tientsin to Hangchow, an 800 mile man-made waterway.

When Ho died, 60,000 men mourned in his funeral procession; it wound around the same streets in which one can walk today. His copper coffin had three compartments, one filled with jade and jewels, one with swords, and between these the body of King Ho. After burial, a terrible white tiger was set to guard his grave: now a tiger of stone stands in the approximate place. This is Tiger Hill.

We visited silk factories and embroidery institutes: silk has been the mainstay of Soochow's existence for hundreds of years. The large needlework screens that I saw were fit for palaces: I wondered to which countries they would be exported. I asked again for prices but again the director begged the question. When I persisted, the director guessed many hundreds of English pounds.

Equally as famous as Soochow's silk are its gardens. Here there are no gaudy beds of color, no pristine trimmed lawns: such staging would detract from the garden's soul! They are, essentially, cloistered areas of retreat, but full of delicate Chinese symbolism. There is a large central pool and around this, suite after suite, the great central house is built. The sleeping quarters, lounging rooms, tea rooms, are joined by long corridors and camel-back bridges. Surrounding the pool are artificially created hills of rock.

In the background are thickets of spindly bamboo, or banks of shrubs for every season of the year. Dwarf pines, trumpet vines and wisteria hang down to the water's edge. The windows are indeed picture windows, so designed that the trapped scene looks like a painting. One of the most famous of these gardens was used by the Japanese as a stable

194

during the occupation. (That night in Soochow we saw the highly popular play about the occupation, *The Red Lantern*. Although we all had earphones for simultaneous translation, the murmurs of anger from the audience during some of the occupation scenes were nonetheless clearly audible.)

I spent a lot of time in this town simply walking around. There is a law forbidding the dumping of refuse into the canals but some do it anyway. They weren't as dirty as those in Venice, however. Women washed in the canals, squatting on the steps, and I wanted to sit with them, but it embarrassed them and after a while I ceased trying. I felt very much alone. The Australians had made some remarks which I, after living outside that country for fifteen years, could not understand and now they, too, were puzzled by my status. Quite innocently they would say in front of Chinese officials:

"You're a bit of a mystery, Lisa, can't make you out."

One of them insisted on making a joke about me being an American and the more I hushed him up the more boisterous he became. It seemed to them, and to me too now, that Yu, Li, or Wang hardly left my side.

Earlier, I had taught Wang *We Shall Overcome*. He had taught me, on one of our many bus rides, a Chinese folk song and this was the only American "folk song" that I knew that was simple enough to teach in return. Now, with some sadness, I noticed he was reluctant to sing it. He was such an open-hearted lad, I knew I had been discussed and now suspicion had come into our simple song-making.

My picture-taking, too, was becoming a marked source of tension. Li asked twice why I took so many pictures of poor conditions and not of good things. I tried to explain that I was not the least interested in rolls of pretty scenery, neither had I made any attempt to photograph only backward conditions. I protested at the unfairness of the accusation, but he kept on:

"So many journalists have come pretending to be friendly

195

and promising to be objective," he said. It sounded just like Yu speaking and then I knew I was under close scrutiny. "Then these films are used to pretend we have done nothing in the past fifteen years."

I said rather stiffly that the Chinese don't have a monopoly on integrity. As soon as I said it I remembered my true position. Nor was I alone in spotting the discrepancy, for the next thing that was said was:

"Then, Lisa, tell us the truth."

I asked what truth.

"That you are an American girl."

I denied it and said I was an Australian, just as my passport said.

"And you live in Sydney, just as your visa application says?"

I told him I admired his astuteness. I suddenly felt I could not lie: his integrity, as well as my own, precluded that. But nor could I, thinking of my husband and sons waiting for me back in San Francisco, tell him the truth although it was hard at that point not to.

"Perhaps you will tell us at the bridge," said Li, not unkindly.

He was referring to the Shumchun bridge at which I would reenter the British New Territories. To wait until then would be an ultimate gesture of distrust.

I started to say something but there was nothing to say. I either told them or I didn't. It was as simple as that.

17

Now we were in Hangchow.

Myra Roper, who was on her third visit to China, had arranged an interview with the leading administrator at Hangchow University. She kindly invited me along. Where time permitted, such interviews could usually be arranged without difficulty. I made few special requests, sought only a couple of interviews myself: I had too many other things on my mind! In this instance, Paul Morawetz came with us; we rode out to the college in a cab with Li, who was to be our interpreter.

It proved to be a fascinating afternoon: never before had I visited any institution in any country where the air of intensity and dedication matched this!

Hangchow University is sixty-eight years old and before Liberation comprised an old-type university with seven separate colleges for physics, business, agriculture, medicine, literature, law, and teachers' training. Now it has nine divisions, three in physical sciences (mathematics, physics, and chemistry) and six in industrial sciences (mechanical, electrical, chemical, civil and radio engineering, and optical instruments).

More than half the student body comes from peasant fam-

197

ilies. Eighteen per cent are girls. The other students comprise teachers and government employees.

I asked the administrator what were the aims of university education, and he promptly replied:

"Education must serve proletarian politics and education must be combined with productive labor."

He added that this meant "all experimentation in the laboratory must be combined with productive labor in the factory."

The factory was on the campus grounds and supplied tools to various industries all over China.

"We do not have degrees. What we have is the actual ability of the student to build socialism. We do grade the students 'good' and 'pass' but that is all. To get into the University they must pass the unified examination of the state. All students take the same examination: only those students who have been counseled to do so in the last year of middle school try for the entrance exam."

I asked what happened to those students who failed to pass the entrance exam.

"Some go to technical schools, some to factories. Most of them like to go to the countryside where culture is needed."

In the rural areas these students, aged about eighteen, would have an education superior to those of most people around them. They would be expected to take an active part in organizing political discussions and study groups, night classes in culture or technical skills, or help the people do artistic things, such as writing poetry or painting.

As for the failure rate:

"It is very small, 2 to 3 per cent. This is a fundamental difference between our society and capitalist society. Our teachers have the responsibility to teach the students well. Our failures are allowed to repeat. If a student fails, although he is really working hard and knows that it is for socialist construction that he is studying, we will continue to give him a chance."

How do middle-school students decide about their future jobs?

"In the third year of middle school (age fifteen) they are counseled. Many make their own choice; the final decision is made by the school according to the student's ability."

I said that I had noticed land under agriculture on the campus.

"That land is worked by outside workers, students don't work any land on this college," the administrator said. "They go away from here, to the distant countryside, and work with the peasants for two weeks."

Where do they do their practical work?

"There is a machine-building factory in this university. Students work there or go to other factories elsewhere that have their specialty. Each specialty follows a different academic calendar. Generally speaking, there are two semesters a year, September to January with three weeks' vacation and the end of February to the middle of July. Then they do their two weeks' work and have six weeks' vacation."

We asked about the students' union and its function.

"The union organizes recreational activities, such as physical education, perhaps a dance, and the wall newspapers." (The wall newspapers, each sheet under a separate pane of glass, under a roofed-over notice board, are to be seen everywhere in China.) The students do not have their own publication. Since the government is whole-heartedly training the students and the students want training there is no question of the union speaking on behalf of the students. Certainly, the students will give opinions as to how to improve the work. It isn't necessary for student unions to speak out their opinions or suggestions. Whenever they have one they can tell anyone concerned. Here there is complete democracy."

"Each class has its own monitor," the administrator said. "This monitor sees to the livelihood of the students, and reflects things to the teacher as far as the students are concerned.

"According to our educational policy, the teacher is not only in charge of teaching but also is responsible for students' study, morals, intelligence, and physical development. The students often have group discussions as part of their study and the teacher will attend such discussions. So the teachers know everyone's opinions. When the students propose a correct idea the teacher will accept it. But if it isn't correct, the teacher will give a correct explanation so that the student will be glad to accept the teacher's viewpoint."

"But suppose they didn't," I asked. I was told that the state needed other workers, particularly in agriculture!

"We are very different from capitalist society," continued the administrator at the point where I had interrupted. "Teachers there go home immediately after class so they do not have close contact with the students. Our teachers are not only responsible for classroom teaching but also for everything else, so there are very close ties.

"Teachers have their own homes on the school ground but are free to go to the dormitories and laboratories at any hour.

"Training here is very concentrated. We have one teacher to six students on an average, but the ratio changes depending what year the student is in. In some fundamental technical classes teachers can give lectures to 100 students."

A foreign language is compulsory for two years, most students take it for three. The most popular are English, Russian, German and Japanese, in that order. The best students in any course are kept on as teachers.

We toured the labs. The equipment was either Chinese, Russian, Czechoslovakian, or German. As we toured the massive factory, where hundreds of students were making tools on various lathes, the administrator remarked:

"Just think! Before Liberation students could only talk!"

There were no tuition or boarding fees. The lights were turned out at 9:50 p.m., students rose at 5:20 a.m. Sunday is a day of rest "but no one has the habit of sleeping all day long," said the administrator.

A stroll through the dormitories—eight wooden bunks with bed rolls to a room—indicated total insulation from any frivolity. In each room every student pored wordlessly over the works of Mao Tse-tung. Obviously, this was their free hour for political studies.

Outside the halls, hundreds of other students, separated by sex for physical education class marched around to the sound of piped-in music. It looked like no university I'd ever seen.

"What about your nonconforming students?" I asked.

"We don't have any," I was told decisively.

This was a vast campus, beautifully laid out and half-ringed with hills. The avenues were all tree-lined, the fields dotted with field and track trainees. Handball players in red T-shirts and white shorts fought a vigorous match. The large amphitheater type of lecture halls with chairs and armrest desks could have been anywhere in the world. The students didn't show any interest in us.

Before returning to our cab we stopped for more tea and talk.

Morawetz, the Australian economist, tried to talk about the lack of the humanities in the students' curriculum. He said he understood that China today must train scientists and perhaps could not afford the luxury of the humanities, but perhaps in another twenty-five years there would be a change in the system.

The reply:

"Your view of it is rather one-sided. Our education policy enables everyone to develop morally, intellectually, and physically. It is not one-sided development. As for the humanities, our understanding is different from yours. Our students do study philosophy, history, and literature.

"According to the law of the development of society, socialist society will replace capitalist society, so that we cannot imagine that after twenty-five years China will change, that China will degenerate, because we have Marxism-Leninism and Chairman Mao's thinking. This is the most scientific law of the development of society."

This conversation took place in a large reception room on the second floor of the administration building. The administrator, in a high-necked navy blue serge tunic, sat erect on a comfortable couch. We sat sunk deep in armchairs, sipping tea: I felt we were all again talking at, and not to, one another. I suggested to Paul Morawetz that we desist, that time was being wasted on both sides. But he persisted.

"Don't confuse change with degeneration," he said flatly. "Capitalism, as Marx knew it, barely existed."

The administrator shifted his position slightly and allowed himself a small smile.

"It is true that in twenty-five years science and technology will develop rapidly, but the fundamental law of the development of society will remain the same. The basic principles of Marxism-Leninism will still be the universal truth and will never be changed."

I was struck by the implications of the administrator's phraseology. The claim that communism contains a universal truth, and an immortal one, and the earlier reference to Mao's "thinking" with its vicarious suggestion of revelation, sounded very much like orthodox religion.

The quotations of the administrator are not written from memory but from the verbatim account that I took, thinking it might be of interest to American college students who would read my newspaper articles.

We drove back to the city. Halfway back, realizing that I

202

had only four days left in China, I decided I would like to walk back along the country roads, but Li flatly refused to tell the driver to stop. In the cobbled, lakeside town of Hangchow, however, he told the driver to pull up and got out himself.

"You should not leave Hangchow before walking to the West Lake," he said. "Come, I will take you."

Everything was still. We found a bench by the lake: there were five minutes to spare before going back. A couple of sampans moved across the lake. Fishermen were hauling in their nets. Everything was gentle: even the air seemed pale and soft. Neither of us spoke and the futility of speech bore in on me. I thought of Li's son and my own sons, boys of the same age and a world apart, and I wondered with a sudden, great feeling of grief what lay ahead for them.

"Do you believe, Li Tieh-fei, all that the administrator said?"

"Oh, yes," he said simply, "all the world will one day be communistic. It might take time but it is surely coming. It is inevitable because we are right."

He spoke in a clear, soft voice, not a boast but what he obviously felt was a flat statement of fact.

We walked back to the hotel, an ultramodern building on the side of a hill with a large marble lobby with glass and greenery, a sort of Hangchow Hilton. I asked Li why China had so firmly shut her doors against so many newspaper reporters.

He said that there were things in China and features of the system that foreigners do not understand.

"But we have never asked that they praise everything they see or like everything. We only ask that we be allowed to run our country in our own way as other countries do without having our accomplishments ignored, or worse, belittled and our ways ridiculed."

All politics and politeness aside, I asked then: did he believe I would be objective.

We were now almost at the hotel lobby, at the end of a winding drive.

He said slowly:

"It is seldom in China that we have the opportunity of making friends with anyone from another country. We meet tourists and businessmen, they come and go constantly. We have become good enough friends, Lisa, for me to be able to tell you that deep in my heart I do not trust you completely."

We looked at each other. Yu stepped out of the elevator and started across to us.

"Come, Lisa," Li jerked his head back in a characteristic gesture, "I feel there is something you still have not told us."

I said this was true, there was something.

I went upstairs to dress for dinner.

18

The following morning

I woke at daybreak and took a fast-paced walk around the lake.

Toward the end of every experience there is an impulse for an accounting: now I had but three days left in China. I had come as a reporter, but now I faced the fact that I could not give an adequate report. China's material progress was visible and measurable but the spirit that made up China's heart and soul was still an imponderable. This spirit rose out of China's ancient past and the present was the harvest of this past: of the future there was no sure telling. But these were big questions for others to answer: all I had wanted to do was to establish a human dialogue with those around me, and I had failed.

This failure filled me with remorse. The inner recesses of the heart and mind are the only sure reality to me: if we cannot communicate one with the other, what then is life? I have no patience with the sentimental notion that people, in the end, are all the same: people are products of their society and societies at this stage in history are as different as fire from ice.

To me, the failure to take into account the realities of man's nature as conditioned by society—the attempt to solve problems with idealistic alternatives that, in fact, do not exist—has been one of the causes for the bloodletting of centuries. The differences in societies, like the color of skin or the shades of flowers, are one of the great gifts of nature. It does not preclude communication; it simply makes the task at once more stimulating and more difficult.

I blamed my failure to win any continuing sense of trust on my own tension and anxiety over my illegal entry. Yet it was evident that others in the group, whose entry into China was legal and who had no political interest, experienced a psychological dislocation similar to my own. The Australians would say kindly, when the Chinese might interpret an innocent remark as a slight: "Oh, well, it doesn't matter, people are different," but there would be a querulous note in their voices and a hint of hurt feelings.

The Chinese are extraordinarily sensitive and with a complex sensitivity that cannot be easily explained. They have, even the humblest of them, vast interior resources of dignity and strength, as if they had been hardened and polished by the rubbings of centuries. Yet on political matters, particularly matters that related to the accomplishments of the Peking regime, they seemed inordinately sensitive and lost to this deep interior strength. Our Western habit of give-and-take argument; our informal, sometimes boisterous manners; our analytic approach to matters of faith, would dissipate this calm. They would say little, but simply withdraw within themselves, leaving just a brittle surface to carry on the functions that politeness demanded. I felt keenly at such times the vast legacy of suspicion and distrust that the West has left in China. They bear us a grudge, a deep grudge, although they say they don't, and it will not be assuaged easily. So it was that toward the end of my stay when I saw anti-American propaganda I thought: Go ahead, sing about it, shout about it, march against it, demonstrate. Express your anger against the West in these ways so that it won't, one day, explode and catch the lot of us.

How had I come to think like this when only three weeks earlier I had entered China, guiltlessly, freely, chuckling with the fun of having gotten a visa illegally? Perhaps because time and time again I was taken aback with the rawness of the emotion that poured out with the slightest provocation. When director Kua of the Viet Namese Friendship Commune spoke of the family who owned "only an iron pot before," his voice was vehement, incredulous: when I stopped to ask students what they wanted to do, their faces would light up like lamps and their voices thrill with expectancy: "Whatever the state wants of me." And when I asked the old lady in the Home of Respect for the Aged what she would be doing now if it hadn't been for the revolution, she cackled aloud with a fierce satisfaction and her watery eyes clouded over and she rocked as she said: "I wouldn't even be alive without the revolution!"

On a more intangible level, there was another cause of the disorientation that not only I was experiencing, but some of those in the group around me. This, perhaps, the larger cause, is the shock of finding oneself caught unexpectedly in the presence of a vast ideal. There is in China an overwhelming social momentum. It pushes against one—even the innocent tourist—catching him, morally and intellectually, in its surge. It is as inescapable as breathing air. It is not the parade, or the banners, or the bands: these are just the trappings. It is a reality, the reality of a revolution whose impetus indeed is growing by what it feeds on. The visitor to China, who cannot see the world and its issues as black and white but as a series of shades of gray, can only stand on the sidelines and wonder what's ahead: and any assessment he makes is sobering and saddening, for the very simplicity of revolution can catch the soul.

I could feel it then myself, a sadness that there was no exploding, motivating force in my own life by which I could play my part in the one imagined stroke which would change the face of the earth! I understood well why those Chinese have returned to their homeland from safe and comfortable positions abroad to embrace the new doctrine and a plain hard life. I understood well why far left and far right causes attract the young. It is the simplicity of the solution offered, the speed, the quick returns: it is a simplicity that makes the slower alternatives offered within a technically advanced society appear limp and ineffectual.

It is also a simplicity so bent on its own ultimate fulfillment, so sure of its "correctness," so determined to avoid the compromises of the past, that it appeared to me to exercise and extend its humanitarianism only to those members of humanity who paid it recognition. I thought of the movie that I had attended the night before—a film on Viet Nam. When shots were shown of dead South Vietnamese government soldiers, some of the Chinese smiled and one laughed outright. Good God! I thought; I feel more strongly about the brotherhood of man than you apparently do. And I said to the one who laughed:

"Why did you laugh? This was just a poor peasant and his life was the only thing he possessed. Perhaps he truly felt he was fighting for a better life, more rice, a little hut. His life was the only thing he possessed and he lost that possession. I do not see that it is funny!"

My statement was received in silence.

I thought, too, of a photographic exhibition in Canton entitled *U.S. Aggressors Get Out of Viet Nam.* Included among its 258 enlarged action shots was one with this caption:

"Cutting out the belly to pluck out the liver."

Reading China's current best-seller, *Letters from South Viet Nam*—a Peking Foreign Language press publication provided free in English and a dozen other languages in every hotel lobby—I learned that American troops like liver and slaughter the Viet Namese to obtain this delicacy. It seemed tragic and incongruous that so much time and effort were being poured into ridding China of the ghosts and superstitions of the past while fostering myths in the present.

Yet, these fragments of fact were only parts of the vast mosaic of China. What was the larger picture that I had glimpsed in my three weeks?

First, no matter how simple it might appear to the Westerner to argue against the validity of "correct thinking," it is not so easy to deny its results. The results, in the six cities I visited, are masses of adequately fed, warm, and cleanly dressed people whose general demeanor is one of dignity and confidence. This, in a nation where it has been reliably estimated that some 300 million persons formerly lived uncertainly from crop to crop on the verge of starvation. The streets are free of the spindle-legged, swollen-bellied children who are part of every other street scene in Southeast Asia. Nor are there any beggars: nor do I know where the beggars have gone. I know that when I asked a doctor in Peking Hospital whether any effort was made to save babies who are hopelessly deformed, mentally or physically, he replied in flawless English and affronted tone: "Our job as doctors is to save life, not take it."

As for Chinese homes, they are often poor, extremely so, by Western standards. The Chinese are highly sensitive about this, as if we had not seen poor homes anywhere else in the world, or as if none of us had come from poor homes ourselves. Yet, these homes were built by past regimes, not the present regime. I saw evidence that indicated the government

209

is doing what it can to put its people into better housing as quickly as possible, a snail's pace by our standards but infinitely more than was accomplished before 1949.

What of personal freedom? As we understand it this means, among other things, the right to strike, to speak, and organize political dissent, to go where, when, and how you want to.

Such freedoms do not exist in China: yet, it is only comparatively recently, with the coming of industrialization, that they have really existed in the West. Certainly, there are large areas of the world in non-Communist countries where these freedoms do not exist. Can the miners of Bolivia, for instance, strike with impunity? Does the Mexican peon, selling his little pile of onions, have the economic freedom to pull up stakes and move some place else? It is only in a few Western countries that the truly poor man has the opportunity to be mobile. These freedoms, dissent and mobility, have never existed in China. Today, even nonconformity appears to be a forbidden luxury. Again, this does not mean that nonconformity of thought does not exist and is not expressed in the pouring out of hearts between friends; but no one is so unwise as to flaunt it publicly.

It was my impression that this pressure to conform sometimes goes against the grain of the intellectual and educated. Yet, it was also my strong impression that these same people —certainly those that I met—are nonetheless willing, and even happy, to make any personal sacrifice required for the fulfillment of the Marxist-Leninist doctrine. Their social consciousness, their feeling of personal responsibility for the welfare of their fellow countryman, seemed to run astonishingly deep and true. I saw many little things that indicated to me that the Chinese officials, at least, are working long hours, getting insufficient rest. They snatched a nap wherever they could on the plane or train: their feelings about the past were just an inch below the surface. They were easily moved to anger and sorrow for things that have been gone for more than a decade. Yet with all the strenuous effort they are making, I detected nothing that would indicate that they would have life any other way. Whatever their own personal frustrations within the system, they appeared to be inevitably measured against the accomplishments of the present, against the benefit accruing to the mass of society.

As for intellectual freedom, there is no historical evidence to indicate that a totalitarian regime destroys the intellect of the Chinese people. The university system in China today would be intolerable to most Westerners: there is nothing to indicate that this is the case with the Chinese student. Indeed, he seems to be thriving in it. As for the outstanding intellectuals, they probably work in China today much as they always have—either accommodating themselves to the system or, in essence, after paying the required tribute, ignoring it.

If freedom as the West understands it is missing in China today, its absence is likely felt as a loss only to a few. It was my impression that the masses are content: their physical and material betterment indicates to them that the government is slowly but surely making good its promise to insure them the right to work, eat, be clothed, and sheltered.

The attitude toward the police, revealing in any country, indicated neither subservience nor intimidation. Well, one might say, but what about the secret police? To that I can only say that virtually all nations today have two police forces, and that I know of no country where the secret police are welcomed; it is impossible for me to say the precise degree to which the Chinese feel themselves scrutinized by "Big Brother."

In effect, it is totally unrealistic not to recognize that, under the Communist regime, the masses of China are not only better off than they were before, but also have freedoms

211

that they have never before experienced, psychological freedoms, not the least of which is freedom from the fear of death by slow starvation.

Now, the reader might say, that is well and good, but what of those who were annihilated to get this order and regime established and in working order? Who is there to speak for them and to say that the price of their lives and property has been worth it? To this I can only ask another question: While such destruction is deplorable, what of the millions who were annihilated or starved to death under other regimes? Perhaps they alone have the right to answer such a question. Certainly, their deaths raised no great outcry in the West.

What of personal conduct? It would be hard to find a society more rigidly puritanical than China is today. Any frivolity, particularly in sexual matters, seems to have withered away under the dictates of "plain living and high thinking."

China asserts its crime rate is minimal and that there is little juvenile delinquency. There is no way of verifying this: yet it is a fact that in Canton, Peking, Shanghai, Wushi, Soochow, and now Hangchow, I could walk the streets at night without fear. Nor did I, nor anyone, bother to lock our hotel rooms night or day: there is no need.

I had left my sunglasses once on the Shanghai train. I told no one of their loss and yet the glasses were returned without comment to my room—150 miles away. Stockings that I had run and tossed into the wastebasket at Soochow were washed and sent ahead to await me in Hangchow.

Paul Morawetz tried for two weeks to get rid of an old pair of brown slacks. He dumped them at airports, on trains and buses and in a succession of hotel rooms. They always showed up, freshly pressed and packaged. Finally, in desperation, he considered dumping them, weighted, into the West Lake in the dead of night.

All these things I thought of, and many, many more, that

morning as I walked around the lake. Now I started back to the hotel and it started to rain. First it was light, a soft, lakeside drizzle, then it tumbled down. I had run from the pavilion across the lawn and into the cobbled street that led up to the hotel. Now it came down too heavy to move in. I crouched in a doorway.

It was a wooden door, with a step curved by feet over the ages, and it opened directly onto the street. I had been there but a moment when it opened and a woman of about my own age opened it. She had a friend with her: both wore wide, black pants and quilted floral jackets. They stared at me in surprise and then motioned me in.

It was gloomy inside, but when they opened the door fully, I could see it was like a kitchen with a stove, cement floor, and little stools on which the women had been sitting while they prepared the greens for dinner. A strange looking, thin-shelled gray crab lay in a woven basket on the floor. A baby, sitting on its stool, started to cry and that made the women laugh. We all laughed and the mother held him and chided him gently. She showed me his little behind and pretended she was giving him a shot. He had been to the doctor, that was why he was crying, she mimed with gestures —never would she admit he was crying because of me! For a while we tried to talk. I drew a map of Australia to show them where I was from and said, Adelaya, the Chinese for Australia, but neither understood and we gave up.

I stayed there for a long while in a companionable quiet and they showed me how they were preparing some vegetables, but they wouldn't let me help. They searched for something to put on my head so I could run on to the hotel, but they were poor. There was nothing surplus in the house, nothing that could be just tossed away and wasted.

Sitting there, the room softly dark and the rain coming down, I thought of how careful one must be to distinguish between what is a human characteristic and what is a characteristic of the system. For instance, my immediate reaction toward the pompous, bureaucratic young official at Hangchow was to attribute these characteristics to the system. But who knows, he might have been a pompous bureaucrat under any system in any country. I thought of the fervor and dedication of the Chinese students: was this being whipped up by Communist pressure—or was it from centuries-old Chinese national pride and love of country? A score of such questions raced through my mind.

Looming larger than all questions, however, was that of my status, and parallel with this, the fear of being detained in China. Admittedly, this fear weighed heavily in my decision not to tell the whole truth. Yet, wasn't it a possibility that I was sacrificing my prime principle both as a human being and as a reporter—that no effort must be spared to communicate with others—through a fear of shadows?

The rain had slackened: I stood at the door. A delivery car went by and my hostess padded out and hailed it. Sure, he would take me up the hill. I jumped in and returned to the hotel with a sense of triumph.

Wang was standing at the entrance of the lobby with a coat on. "Good," he said, "I was just going to look for you!"

Later that night, after another movie—this one on the October 1 National Day Parade—I hailed Li to one side and told him I wanted to talk to him. We walked out to the terrace. It was a warm night and people were talking and strolling all around us.

Now that the moment had come I felt scared, for once it was said there was no retracting it. When I spoke my mouth was dry.

I said that I was a reporter on the staff of the San Francisco *Examiner*. I lived in America, my husband was an American and so were my sons. They did not have dual citizenship:

214

I had lied. I had told other lies, but they were all relating to my visa application. Everything else was the truth.

I looked up: Li seemed to be looking through my eyes into my soul.

"Why did you do it?"

I sought desperately for unadulterated honesty.

"It wasn't because I have any particular love for China," I said. "If South America was closed down to outside visitors, or any other country, I would have had the same desire as a newspaper reporter to get in and see what was going on. Yet —it isn't only that I was curious. I have wanted to come here for many years: once, years ago, I saw a picture of your people on their knees nibbling grass and an old man nearby gnawing the bark off a tree. I have never forgotten it. I was curious to see what the Communists had done. When you exploded your first atom bomb it somehow became, to me personally, almost imperative: it changed everything. You weren't just quaint little Orientals any longer, willing to live on the smell of an oil rag. Overnight you became a threat and in America that's about all we know about you. As long as we don't know you as human beings, we will fear and hate you, and you us. It is easy to bomb and burn statistics but not so easy to kill other human beings."

Li looked as if a thousand thoughts within him were battling for supremacy. He continued to look intently at me: then he said, as if to clean up one final doubt:

"You did not have to come, your company did not make you?"

I said no, that such a thing would not be possible, that I had free choice to refuse such an assignment. I said then that I was frightened, that I did not consider myself of any importance, but that the question of American journalists visiting China was a very contentious issue. I did not know how seriously Peking authorities would view my entry. I made it clear

215

that I had spoken to Li realizing he would report immediately to Yu.

"And why have you told us now?"

It sounded so heroic and grand that I couldn't help but grin. Yet when I came to say it my voice came out as if in tears. I said, some of us, from your country and from mine, at some level, away from an official table in Europe, must start talking to each other as members of the human race.

"I wanted once, before I left, to talk to you, not as an American newspaper reporter, not with any barriers of duplicity between us, but just as one human being to another. This is my only chance: I must forget the cost and take it. We live within ten hours' flight time from one another, Li Tieh-fei, yet I will never see you again, nor Yu nor Wang, nor your fair country."

My greatest fear I kept to myself: that time is running out, that things were getting under way that can't be stopped; that this wall of silence one day might well end with my sons and his in bloody battle.

Li was silent with his own thoughts.

Then he said simply:

"Thank you, Lisa. I assure you, I could guarantee, nothing will happen to you."

The next day passed in the lazy serenity of spring. The morning mist lay around the lake until noon when it lifted to disclose the mountains on the other side. The fishermen set their nets. The women opened their wooden doorways and called to each other across the cobbled streets. It could have been a thousand years ago.

It was not until we were in the train to Shumchun that Yu broached the subject of what he called my mistake. I could hear his voice: my eyes watched the countryside slipping away as I slid back toward Hong Kong.

"We are truly grateful to you for your honesty," I heard

him say, "but governments do have regulations. We do not want American journalists here. Those who came years ago seemed to be friendly but they lied about us."

He was as fresh and as peppy as the day we had started: I noticed him counting heads as we boarded the train at Canton just as he had counted them that morning that now seemed long ago. Had it been only three weeks? I watched the rice paddies slither by, glistening now in the sun, the coolies still bent over them as if they hadn't moved in centuries. An old Chinese expression sprung to mind: "Where the cart has passed, there are tracks in the mud."

I asked Yu why no action had been taken against me, and he promptly declared it was because I was "a representative of the American people, who are our friends, and not of the American government."

At Shumchun station, we shook hands and again I promised "the people of China" that I would tell the truth about them fairly and objectively. Yu, a different Yu now, no longer smiling and no longer the peasant, instead a mass of raw intensity, said he indeed hoped I would tell "the truth of what you have seen, just as Anna Louise Strong believes you will."—it was the first and only time that my visit to Miss Strong had been mentioned—and that is simply all I have tried to do.

Final farewells in this life are not easy. In moments the doors of China would be closed against me and might never be reopened. I stood at the Shumchun bridge, flight bag in hand, feeling the sun and the silence. The Hong Kong official in the middle of the bridge already held my passport: I could see him waiting. I shook hands all around. I reached out for another bag: it seemed someone had my hand. A voice said: "Remember us, Lisa," and I walked away.

In the middle of the bridge I turned to look back but all I could see were three blurred figures with their hands raised in farewell and China already dimming in the background.

About the Author

Lisa Hobbs was born in Melbourne, Australia, and educated in Australia, Europe, and the U.S.A. She holds a degree in sociology and has been a newspaper reporter since 1948. Her work as foreign correspondent included two years in London and special assignments in Asia prior to joining the staff of the San Francisco Examiner five years ago. Married in 1950, she lives in San Francisco with her husband, a teacher, and their two sons.